IN THE
HEAVENLIES

Practical Expository Addresses

on the

Epistle to the Ephesians

by

H. A. IRONSIDE, LITT.D.

Pastor MOODY MEMORIAL CHURCH, Chicago.

Reprinted from "The Moody Church News."

LOIZEAUX BROTHERS
Neptune, New Jersey

FIRST EDITION, DECEMBER 1937
THIRTEENTH PRINTING, FEBRUARY 1970

PUBLISHED BY LOIZEAUX BROTHERS, Inc.
*A Nonprofit Organization, devoted to the Lord's Work
and to the Spread of His Truth*

PRINTED IN THE UNITED STATES OF AMERICA

CONTENTS

4 Contents

PREFATORY NOTE

This volume consists of addresses delivered through several months in the Moody Memorial Church of Chicago, and stenographically reported. They have been considerably abbreviated and repetitions omitted, but nothing essential has been changed. It is hoped that they may prove helpful to many, by opening up new vistas of truth and practically applying truth already known.

H. A. IRONSIDE.

July, 1937.
Chicago, Ill.

THE SPHERE
OF CHRISTIAN PRIVILEGE

✦ ✦ ✦

"Paul, an apostle of Jesus Christ by the will of God, to the saints which are at Ephesus, and to the faithful in Christ Jesus: Grace be to you, and peace, from God our Father, and from the Lord Jesus Christ. Blessed be the God and Father of our Lord Jesus Christ, who hath blessed us with all spiritual blessings in heavenly places in Christ" (Eph. 1:1-3).

✦ ✦ ✦

THERE is nothing redundant in God's Word. Men write books and very frequently pad them in order to give quantity as well as quality, but there is nothing like that in the Bible. God's words are tried—"as silver tried in a furnace of earth, purified seven times"—and therefore we may well give our most careful attention to every item and every expression used.

With what great outstanding theme does this epistle deal? It opens up the truth of the privileges and responsibilities of the Church as the Body and Bride of Christ. It brings before us our position as believers; as quickened, raised, and seated in Christ in heavenly places.

There are very remarkable correspondences between certain Old Testament books and New Testament epistles. The Epistle to the Romans, for instance, answers to Exodus; the Letter to the Hebrews is the counterpart of Leviticus; and this Epistle to the Ephesians is the New Testament book of Joshua. In Joshua we have the people of Israel entering upon the possession of their inheritance. In Ephesians believers are called upon to enter by faith now into the possession of that inheritance which we shall enjoy in all its fulness by-and-by. We are far richer than we realize. All things are ours, and yet how little we appropriate! It is said in the prophecy of Obadiah that when the Lord returns and His kingdom is established, the people of Israel shall "possess their possessions." This is a challenge to us. Do you possess your possessions? Or are your heavenly estates like castles in Spain about which you dream, but never really make your own? I trust the Spirit of God may lead us into the present enjoyment of our portion in Christ.

For our purpose the epistle may be divided very simply, without breaking it up into many portions which would be difficult to carry in our memories. We shall divide it into two parts, the first three chapters giving us the doctrinal unfolding, and the last three, the practical outcome;

the first division gives us our inheritance, and the last, the behavior that should characterize those who are so richly blessed. That is the divine order; instruction in the truth first, practice in accordance with the truth afterwards. Now let us look particularly at these opening verses.

We are struck at once by the name of the writer, Paul. Thirteen New Testament epistles begin with the word "Paul." Another one is undoubtedly from Paul, but begins with the magnificent word "God." I refer to the Epistle to the Hebrews. Do we stop to inquire as often as we should how this man ever came to be called Paul? That was not his name originally. His name in the first place was Saul. He was a Benjamite, and bore the name of the first king, who came from the tribe of Benjamin. For many years this man was a haughty, self-righteous Pharisee, proud of his genealogy, of his religion, of his personal devotedness, until one day he had a meeting with our Lord Jesus Christ. Have you had such a meeting? From that moment on everything was changed for him. He could say:

> "I was journeying in the noon-tide,
>   When His light shone o'er my road;
> And I saw Him in the glory,
>   Saw Him, Jesus, Son of God.
>
> Marvel not that Christ in glory
>   All my inmost soul hath won;
> I have seen a light from heaven,
>   Far beyond the brightest sun."

It was that vision of Christ that changed Saul the Pharisee, into Paul, the humble, lowly servant of Christ. He did not use the new name immediately, you remember. It seems to have been taken after he won his first outstanding Gentile convert in the Isle of Cyprus—after the conversion of Sergius Paulus; and it appears to have been given him in recognition of his apostolic ministry. It means "the little one," a wonderful name for one who once thought himself so great; but that is what Christ does for one. "What things were gain to me, those I counted loss for Christ. Yea, doubtless, and I count all things but loss for the excellency of the knowledge of Christ Jesus my Lord: for whom I have suffered the loss of all things, and do count them but dung, that I may win Christ" (Phil. 3: 7, 8). All that Saul gloried in, Paul flung away for Jesus' sake; and he was content to be little, "less than the least of all saints," that in him Christ Jesus might show forth all long-suffering.

I remember going to a colored camp-meeting, and the dear black folk were singing a little ditty that went like this:

> "The quickest way up is down,
>   The quickest way up is down;
> You may climb up high, and try and try,
>   But the quickest way up is down."

How long it takes some of us to learn that! We are always trying to become somebody, and

forgetting that, "Whosoever will save his life
shall lose it: and whosoever will lose his life,"
says Jesus, "for My sake shall find it" (Matt.
16:25). Blessed it is when the princely Saul
becomes the little Paul as he bows at the Saviour's
feet.

Paul calls himself an apostle. Just what is an
apostle? The word might be translated "a messenger," "a sent one," "one sent on a mission,"
and so there is a certain sense in which every
missionary is an apostle. But there is a higher
sense in which the word "apostle" refers to those
who were specially commissioned by our Lord
Jesus Christ to go forth in the world and carry
the truth through which the Church was instituted. Paul was not among those who knew the
Lord on earth, but he was ordained an apostle
to the nations by His personal appointment
when the risen Christ appeared to him that day
on the Damascus turnpike. He said to him, "I
have appeared unto thee for this purpose, to
make thee a minister and a witness both of these
things which thou hast seen, and of those things
in the which I will appear unto thee" (Acts 26:
16). And so Paul could go forth, the apostle of
the Lord Jesus Christ, saying:

> "Christ the Son of God hath sent me
>   Through the midnight lands;
> Mine the mighty ordination
>   Of the piercéd hands."

He was an apostle of Jesus Christ by the will of God.

I do not like to touch upon critical questions in connection with these studies, and yet I must do so here. Some people do not notice divine names carefully, and that is the reason why those who copied the manuscripts were not always particular whether they wrote "Jesus Christ," or "Christ Jesus," but here it should be "Christ Jesus." Peter, James, John, and Jude spoke of our blessed Lord as "Jesus Christ." Why? Because "Jesus" is His human name and in resurrection He was made Lord and Christ. They knew Him on earth as "Jesus," the self-humbled One. But Paul never knew Him in that way; he never knew Him as "Jesus" on earth; he had his first sight of Him in the glory, and his soul was so thrilled with what he beheld that he never thought of Him as other than the glorified One. So he invariably writes in the original text, "Christ Jesus," and his message is in a peculiar sense called "The gospel of the glory." The other disciples walked with Him on earth, and delighted to dwell on what He was when here, and so they speak of Him as "Jesus Christ." Any critical version will make this distinction clear.

Paul is a messenger, a sent one of Christ Jesus "by the will of God." It was no mere idle thought of his that sent him forth on this mission. It was not that he concluded it would be the best way to spend his life. He who saved him commissioned him, and sent him forth to be a teacher of the Gentiles in faith and verity; and so he insists on the divine character of his commission, "An apostle of Christ Jesus by the will of God."

A simple cobbler was being introduced to a rather dignified clergyman, and when the cobbler said, "I didn't get your name," the clergyman replied, "The Reverend Doctor Blank, by the will of God." The cobbler said, "And I am John Doe, cobbler by the will of God; I am glad to meet you, sir." It is a great thing, whatever your station in life may be, to recognize it as "by the will of God." Am I a preacher of the gospel? It should be only because I have heard a divine call urging me forth and thrusting me out. Am I a merchant? Has it been given to me to make money for the glory of God? Then let me remember that I am a merchant by the will of God, and I should be sure that I am where God's will has placed me, and should seek to be faithful to Him.

The apostle addresses himself, though not to two classes of people as one might suppose, "To the saints which are at Ephesus, and to the faithful in Christ Jesus." That might suggest that the term "saints" took in all believers and that "the faithful" included a spiritual aristocracy, but it might better be rendered, "To the saints which are at Ephesus, even the believers in Christ Jesus." In other words, it is faith in Christ Jesus which constitutes a person a saint. Are you a saint? You say, "I wouldn't like to go so far. I am not sinless yet." A saint is not a sinless person; a saint is a separated person, separated to God in Christ Jesus. People have an idea that if you live a very saintly life, eventually you may become a saint. God says, "Do you believe in My Son? Have you trusted Him? Very well, then, I constitute you a saint; be sure that you live in a saintly way." We do not become saints by saintliness, but we should be characterized by saintliness because we are saints.

In verse 2 we have the apostolic salutation, "Grace be to you, and peace, from God our Father, and from the Lord Jesus Christ." He is not referring at all to the grace that saves. These people were already saved. He tells them, "By grace are ye saved through faith; and that not of yourselves: it is the gift of God: not of works, lest any man should boast" (Eph. 2:8, 9). It is a great thing to have that settled. So many of us never seem to get anything settled. We come to Christ, but lack positive conviction and definite assurance. That comes out in a great many of the hymns we sing. How hard it is to get hymns that are absolutely scriptural. In a meeting some time ago I was giving a message on "The Indwelling Holy Spirit." At the close of the service, the dear pastor stood up and said, "In the light of this splendid address, let us sing, 'Holy Spirit, faithful Guide, ever near the Christian's side,'" and I felt my heart sink as I thought, "After I have spent forty minutes trying to show them that the Holy Spirit is not merely at our side, but dwells in us, they haven't got it yet." Then they came to that last gloomy verse, and I said, "Please don't sing such words as these:

> " 'When our days of toil shall cease,
>   Waiting still for sweet release;
>   Nothing left but heaven and prayer,
>   Wond'ring if our names are there;
>   Wading deep the dismal flood,
>   Pleading nought but Jesus' blood.' "

What a mixture! I refuse to sing it. I *know* my name is there!

I do not understand how it is that Christians are so slow in laying hold of divine truth. Here in our verse the apostle means grace to keep, to preserve us, not grace to save. For the believer that is already settled for eternity, but we need daily grace for daily trials.

How does one obtain this grace? "We have not an high priest which cannot be touched with the feeling of our infirmities; but was in all points tempted like as we are, yet without sin. Let us therefore come boldly unto the throne of grace, that we may obtain mercy, and find grace to help in time of need" (Heb. 4:15, 16). We were saved by grace, we began with grace, but we need grace every step of the way that we might triumph over the world and over the natural propensities of our poor hearts; for as Christians we have the nature of the old man in us still, and it will readily manifest itself if not subdued and kept in place by grace divine.

"Grace be to you, and peace." This is not peace *with* God which was made for us by the blood of Calvary's cross. Every believer in the Lord Jesus should know what it is to have peace with God, "Being justified by faith, we have peace with God through our Lord Jesus Christ" (Rom. 5:1). But this is the peace *of* God, garrisoning our hearts as we move along toward our heavenly home, the same peace that filled the heart of Jesus when here on earth. May I use an illustration of Dr. W. I. Carroll's right here? Jesus said to His disciples in the ship, "Let us go over to the other side." Where were they going? To the other side. When they got into the boat, He went to sleep in perfect peace, and in the middle of the night the elements raged, the devil stirred up a terrific tempest, but it could not drown Him. It was impossible that the boat in which He sailed should founder; but the disciples were terrified and they aroused that Holy Sleeper and said, "Master, carest Thou not that we perish?" Jesus, wakened from His sleep, looked at them, and said, "O ye of little faith." Little faith! With the thunder roaring, the lightning flashing, the wind blowing a gale, and the sea raging, why, you surely could not blame men for being afraid! But you see, Jesus did not say to them, "Let us go out into the middle of the lake and get drowned." He said, "Let us go over to the other side," and they should have rested on His word. They would have had the same peace that He had if they had believed His word.

Do the trials of the way sometimes test your soul? Do you wonder what will become of you? This is what will become of you: If worst comes to worst and you starve to death, you are going Home to heaven! Thousands of people are dying and going to a lost eternity, but no matter what comes to you, if you are saved, you are going Home! As we realize that we are in His hand, the peace of God, like a military garrison, keeps our hearts and saves us from all doubt and fear.

"Grace be to you, and peace, from God our Father." Do you love to dwell on those words, "From God our Father"? The blessed Lord came to reveal the Father, and the Holy Spirit gives us to know the Father, and one of the first evidences that a man is born of God is that he lifts his heart to heaven and says, "Father." This is a different thing from the God of the

Lodge Hall, from the God of the Modernist, from
the doctrine of the universal Fatherhood of God
and brotherhood of man. That is not what the
apostle is talking about. He has been addressing
saints, believers in Christ Jesus, and when he
speaks to them, he says, "God our Father." It
is only by regeneration, only by the second birth,
that we enter into this blessed relationship.
Scripture declares that those who have never
been regenerated are of the flesh, they are not
the children of God, and our Lord Jesus said to
certain ones, "Ye are of your father the devil,
and the lusts of your father ye will do" (John
8:44). That does not sound very much like the
universal Fatherhood of God and the brotherhood of man! People tell me that is what Jesus
came to teach. I defy anyone to find any such
thing anywhere in all the teaching of our Lord
Jesus Christ. He said to Nicodemus, "Except a
man be born again, he cannot see the kingdom
of God" (John 3:3). In that very verse He
denies the universal Fatherhood of God and
brotherhood of man. I know all men are brothers
in Adam and we are one in sin, but it is only
by a new birth that I become a brother of the
saints and a child of God.

"Grace be to you, and peace, from God our
Father, and from the Lord Jesus Christ." How
the Holy Ghost delights to give Him His full
title, "the Lord Jesus Christ." He is Lord of all,

and therefore all men are called upon to subject themselves to Him. Notice verse 3, for in this we properly begin the study of the epistle: "Blessed be the God and Father of our Lord Jesus Christ." He has said before that God is our Father, and now points out that in a peculiar sense God sustains that relationship to the Lord Jesus Christ. He is the God of our Lord Jesus Christ because Jesus became Man, and as Man He looks up to the Father as His God. He is the Father of our Lord Jesus Christ because Christ is God the Son from all eternity. What a wealth of instruction is bound up in that expression, "The God and Father of our Lord Jesus Christ." It was not until the resurrection that He revealed this blessed relationship. He said to Mary, "Go to My brethren, and say unto them, I ascend unto My Father, and your Father, and to My God, and your God" (John 20:17). He does not say, "I ascend to *our* God and *our* Father." His relationship is different to ours. He was not simply a man brought into union with God, but He was the Son of God, come down to earth in grace, who became Man for our redemption.

Farther on in this epistle there are two prayers, one in the last part of this chapter, and the other in chapter three, and they accord in a very striking way with these titles. In chapter 1:17 Paul prays that "the God of our Lord Jesus

Christ" may do certain things; and then when we turn over to chapter 3: 14 we read, "For this cause I bow my knees unto the Father of our Lord Jesus Christ." Why the difference? Because in the first prayer he is speaking of the divine counsels and power, and so he addresses himself to God. In the second prayer he takes into consideration our relationship to God and addresses himself to "the Father of our Lord Jesus Christ." Scripture is wonderfully accurate.

"Blessed be the God and Father of our Lord Jesus Christ, who hath blessed us with all spiritual blessings in heavenly places in Christ." Notice, "He *hath* blessed us." The apostle is not speaking of something that may be ours when we get to heaven, but right here and now I have been blessed with every spiritual blessing in Christ Jesus. People often ask me if I have obtained the second blessing yet, and I generally say, "Second blessing? Why, I am somewhere up in the hundreds of thousands as far as that goes, if you refer to experience; but actually I obtained every blessing that God has for a redeemed sinner when I put my trust in the Lord Jesus Christ." He does not just give us a little now and a little later, but gives us everything in Christ. It is all yours. Enter into it and enjoy it. It is one thing to have the blessings and another thing to make them yours. I read recently about a man in Montana for whom search had long been made. Some years ago a British noble-man died, leaving an estate which, as he had no children, would go to the nearest heir. This man away out west was the nearest heir, living in pov-erty, and just eking out a struggling existence when they found him and gave him the news that the estate was his. It was his all the time, but he did not know it. What did he do when he found it out? Did he say, "Well, it is a good thing to know that I have something to fall back on and some day I will go and look into it?" No, he went down town, and on the strength of it bought himself a new suit and a ticket, and started to Great Britain. I read an interview which the reporters had with him. They said, "Where are you going?" He answered, "To take possession of my estate." You and I are richer far than he was, but do we really take possession by faith of the things that are ours in Christ?

You may say, "But name some of these things that are ours." He has blessed us with the bless-ing of forgiveness of our sins, with justification from all things, with sanctification in Christ, with a robe of perfect righteousness, with a heavenly citizenship, by giving us a place in the Body of Christ, by making us heirs of His riches in Christ Jesus! And yet how some of us struggle along, eking out a poor, wretched, miserable existence! We act as spiritual paupers when we ought to be living like millionaires.

"Who hath blessed us with all spiritual blessings in heavenly places in Christ." God has
made Christ Jesus to be unto us wisdom, righteousness, sanctification, and redemption, and yet
for six years after I was converted I was still
seeking righteousness and sanctification. But
one day I woke up to the fact that it was all
mine in Christ Jesus, and that I had simply to
appropriate and enjoy it.

Now notice he says, "In heavenly places." My
blessings are all yonder, and He calls me in the
Spirit to rise to my heavenly citizenship and live
in this world as a heavenly man should live, drawing from the glory all the resources I need that
I may be more than conqueror day by day, as
I pass through this scene.

Notice how carefully you have to read Scripture. "Who hath blessed us with all spiritual
blessings in heavenly places in Christ." What a
mistake it would be to translate that, "with
Christ." Do you see the difference? How often
we hear people misquote it, and say, "He hath
raised us up together, and made us sit together
in heavenly places *with* Christ Jesus." Nothing
of the kind. We are not seated together *with*
Christ; we are seated *in* Him. He is there as
our representative, and that is an altogether different thing from being seated *with* Him. We
have "everything *in* Jesus and Jesus everything!"
Mark, this does not mean that we are only

blessed and seated together in Christ when we
have a real, good, happy, spiritual meeting. Sometimes when we have a good meeting and the people think they have been helped, some well-mean-
ing brother closes in prayer and says, "O Lord,
we thank Thee that we have been sitting together
in heavenly places in Christ Jesus this morning."
I say to myself, "The dear brother hasn't got it
yet. He thinks because there is a glow in his
heart, because he feels happy, that means he is
sitting in heavenly places in Christ." But I am
sitting in heavenly places in Christ just as truly
when I am oppressed with the trials of the way,
as I am when I am flourishing and have everything that heart could desire. It is a question of
fact: Christ is there in the heavenlies, and God
sees me in Him. I am blessed in Him and all
the treasures of heaven are at my disposal, and
I am to draw upon them as I have need in order
that I may be happy, in order that I may rejoice
as I go forth in His service down here.

OUR ELECTION
AND PREDESTINATION

✓ ✓ ✓

"According as He hath chosen us in Him before the foundation of the world, that we should be holy and without blame before Him." (Put the stop right there.) "In love having predestinated us unto the adoption of children by Jesus Christ to Himself, according to the good pleasure of His will" (Eph. 1: 4, 5).

✓ ✓ ✓

IN verse 3 the apostle gives thanks to "The God and Father of our Lord Jesus Christ"—the Source of all our blessings—"who hath blessed us with all spiritual blessings in heavenly places in Christ." And now he carries our minds back to the past eternity that we may be brought to realize that salvation is altogether of God, not at all of ourselves. An old hymn puts it this way:

> "'Tis not that I did choose Thee,
> For, Lord, that could not be,
> This heart would still refuse Thee,
> But Thou hast chosen me."

And again in another that we know well, we are taught to sing:

"Jesus sought me when a stranger
　Wand'ring from the fold of God;
He to rescue me from danger
　Interposed His precious blood."

It was God Himself who purposed our salvation in the past eternity. It is Jesus Christ who wrought out our salvation upon the cross when the fulness of time had come. It is God the Holy Spirit who convicts us and brings us to repentance and to a saving knowledge of the grace of God as revealed in Christ. We cannot take any credit to ourselves for our salvation. A little boy was asked, "Have you found Jesus?" He looked up and said, "Please, sir, I didn't know He was lost; but I was, and He found me." We did not have to do the seeking after Him, He sought us because of the love that was in His heart from eternity.

"According as He hath chosen us in Him before the foundation of the world." This, of course, is the truth of election. Again and again believers are spoken of as elect people, as children chosen of God. Mr. Spurgeon said, "God certainly must have chosen me before I came into this world or He never would have done so afterwards." He set His love upon us in the past eternity. This troubles people sometimes; and yet how could it be otherwise? God who is infinite in wisdom, with whom the past and the future are all one eternal *now*, purposed in His heart before the world came into existence, that He was going to have a people who would be to the praise and glory of His grace for all eternity, and He looked down through the ages and saw us as those for whom He would give His Son in order to add to the glory of the Lord Jesus Christ. It is wonderful to see how intimately the joy of Christ and our salvation are linked together. John Bunyan said, "Oh, this Lamb of God! He had a whole heaven to Himself, myriads of angels to do His bidding, but these could not satisfy Him. He must have sinners to share it with Him."

You notice in verse 3 he uses the double title, "The God and Father of our Lord Jesus Christ." It is God who purposes it this way, it is God who plans, it was God who chose us in Christ before the foundation of the world; and, notice, it is not that He chose the Church as such, but He chose every individual who was to be a member of that Church, to be one with Christ for eternity. You say, "I do not understand that." I don't either. Whenever I come to consider a subject like this, God's electing grace and predestinating love, I remind myself that the Word says, "My thoughts are not your thoughts, neither are your ways My ways, saith the Lord. For as the heavens are higher than the earth, so are My ways higher than your ways, and My thoughts than your thoughts" (Isa. 55:8, 9). But it may help us a little if we consider this apart from the question of the fall of man.

Before the world was made, before sin came in, God chose us in Christ to be with His Son for all eternity. The fact that sin came in did not alter God's purpose. He is still going to carry it out in spite of all that Satan has done to wreck His fair creation. The purpose of God is according to His grace, grace to those who could not earn it, who did not deserve anything but eternal judgment. Somebody has well said, "The truth of election is a family secret." It is not something that we go out and proclaim to the world. We read, "Cast not your pearls before swine," and swine, you know, are unclean. We are not to go to unsaved men in the uncleanness of their sin and talk about election. They would not understand it at all; but it is a family secret that God loves to whisper in the ears of His beloved children.

It has been pictured in this way. Here is a vast host of people hurrying down the broad road with their minds fixed upon their sins, and one stands calling attention to yonder door, the entrance into the narrow way that leads to life eternal. On it is plainly depicted the text, "Whosoever will, let him come." Every man is invited, no one need hesitate. Some may say, "Well, I may not be of the elect, and so it would be useless for me to endeavor to come, for the door will not open for me." But God's invitation is absolutely sincere: it is addressed to every man, "Whosoever

will, let him take of the water of life freely"
(Rev. 22:17). If men refuse to come, if they
pursue their own godless way down to the pit,
whom can they blame but themselves for their
eternal judgment? The messenger addressed
himself to all, the call came to all, the door could
be entered by all, but many refused to come and
perished in their sins. Such men can never blame
God for their eternal destruction. The door was
open, the invitation was given, they refused, and
He says to them sorrowfully, "Ye will not come
unto Me, that ye might have life." But see, as
the invitation goes forth, every minute or two
some one stops and says, "What is that?" "The
way to life," is the reply. "Ah, that I might find
the way to life! I have found no satisfaction in
this poor world." We read, "She that liveth in
pleasure is dead while she liveth." "I should
like to know how to be free from my sin, how to
be made fit for the presence of God." And such
an one draws near and listens, and the Spirit of
God impresses the message upon his heart and
conscience and he says, "I am going inside: I will
accept the invitation; I will enter that door," and
he presses his way in and it shuts behind him.
As he turns about he finds written on the inside
of the door the words, "Chosen in Christ before
the foundation of the world." "What!" he says,
"had God His heart fixed on me before ever the
world came into being?" Yes, but he could not

find it out until he got inside. You see, you can pass the door if you will, you can trample the love of God beneath your feet, you can spurn His grace if you are determined to do it, but you will go down to the pit and you will be responsible for your own doom.

There is no such thing taught in the Word of God as predestination to eternal condemnation. If men are lost, they are lost because they do not come to Christ. When men do come to Christ, they learn the wonderful secret that God has foreknown it all from eternity, and that He had settled it before the world came into existence that they were to share the glory of His Son throughout endless ages. D. L. Moody used to say in his quaint way, when people talked about the subject of election, "The whosoever wills are the elect, and the whosoever won'ts are the non-elect." And so you can settle it for yourself whether you will be among the elect of God or not.

When asked to explain the doctrine of election a colored brother once said, "Well, it's this way, the Lord done voted for my salvation; the devil done voted for my damnation; and I done voted with the Lord, and so we got into the majority." The devil seeks my eternal loss and God seeks my eternal blessing, and my heart says, "I will." I then know that I am among those chosen in Christ before the foundation of the world. Let

me link this up with another scripture, 2 Thess.
2:13, "But we are bound to give thanks always
to God for you, brethren, beloved of the Lord,
because God hath from the beginning chosen you
to salvation through sanctification of the Spirit
and belief of the truth." There you have the purpose of God in the past eternity. God had from
the beginning chosen you unto salvation, and He
is carrying out His purpose through the work of
the Holy Spirit and belief of the truth on the part
of the one who hears the message.

Then again listen to the Apostle Peter, "Elect
according to the foreknowledge of God the
Father, through sanctification of the Spirit, unto
obedience and sprinkling of the blood of Jesus
Christ: Grace unto you, and peace, be multiplied"
(1 Pet. 1:2). There you have exactly the same
order. God the Father foreknew us from eternity,
but it was up to us whether or not we would
yield to Christ. When we did yield in the obedience of faith, we took our places beneath the
sprinkled blood of Jesus and our salvation was
eternally assured. People try sometimes to put
the whole responsibility upon God and say, "If
God has not chosen me, I cannot be saved." If
you will trust in Christ, you may know that God
has chosen you.

You remember that striking illustration which
the Spirit of God Himself gives us in the last of
the book of Acts. When Paul and his company

were on their way to Rome, a terrific storm arose, and they were casting out some of the cargo in order to lighten the ship, but finally they gave up in despair. And then an angel appeared and spoke with Paul, and Paul called for the captain of the ship and said, "Be of good cheer: for there shall be no loss of any man's life among you, but of the ship. For there stood by me this night the angel of God, whose I am, and whom I serve, saying, Fear not, Paul; thou must be brought before Caesar: and, lo, God hath given thee all them that sail with thee" (Acts 27: 22-24). There was God's foreknowledge. Every one in that ship would be brought through safely, they would all land in Italy, not one of them would be lost. But a little while afterwards Paul noticed something going on among the sailors. They were fitting out a boat and were preparing to launch it into the sea, putting some provisions into it and getting ready to cut away and leave the ship. And Paul said to the captain, "Except these abide in the ship, ye cannot be saved" (Acts 27: 31). Had he not already told them that none should perish? That was God's side. Then he said, "Except these abide in the ship, ye cannot be saved"—that was their side. They were responsible to see that no one left the ship, and so it is in regard to the doctrine of election and man's responsibility. Every one who is saved will be in heaven because he was chosen in Christ before the foundation of the world, and yet every man who is ever saved will be there because as a poor guilty sinner he put his personal trust in the Lord Jesus Christ. You may say, "I can't harmonize this." You do not need to do so; just believe it and go on your way rejoicing.

Look a little farther, "According as He hath chosen us in Him before the foundation of the world, that we should be holy and without blame before Him." God, who foresaw all who would put their trust in Christ, provided a means whereby all our sin and iniquity could be settled for, in order that we might be presented holy and without blame before Him. This, of course, involves the work of the cross. Redemption was not an after thought with God, it was all provided for when He decided to bring into existence creatures who could give Him voluntary love and service.

The question may be asked, "Why did not God who knows all things create a race of people who could not have sinned, who could not have spurned Him nor hated Him, but who would always have done that which was right in His sight, who would always have loved and obeyed Him? Is not God in some sense responsible for sin because He created a creature weak enough to sin? Could He not have created one so strong that he could not have sinned?" Certainly He could. He could have made creatures that could not have failed Him. He has given us samples of this in the lower world. He has made creatures who never deviate one hair's breadth from the purpose of their being. Dr. Leander Keyser, who is not only a great theologian, but a great naturalist, says, "I have studied birds for over forty years and have had thousands of them under my observation, and I say to the honor of the bird kingdom that I have never known an unchaste bird." Do you see what that means? God makes those little feathered creatures to act according to His own thought for them. Think of the Mourning Dove who, if it loses its mate, remains widowed all of its life. God has constituted it that way, and could have so constituted mankind that they could not have deviated from the path of rectitude. But the determination to create a man or woman who could give Him loyal obedience, loving service, and voluntary devotion, necessitated the creation of men and women who could turn away from God if they wanted to, refuse to obey Him if they so desired. Otherwise there would have been no freedom in their love, devotion, reverence, and affection, and God was willing to take all the risk that He did take in order to have beings in this universe who would give Him glad and free-hearted love and devotion. So when sin came in, the Saviour was given, and the Seed of the woman has bruised the serpent's head and now, through the work of Christ,

God can present us in His glorious presence holy and without blame in Him. It is not what we are naturally in ourselves, but what we are in Christ Jesus.

Now notice in verse 5 we have another word that troubles people. We read, "In love having predestinated us." You will notice that I began reading verse 5 with the last part of verse 4. I put the period after the word "Him"—"That we should be holy and without blame before Him." Our Authorized Version puts it this way, "That we should be holy and without blame before Him in love," but there is something deeper than that. I read it, "That we should be holy and without blame before Him," and then start the next clause, "In love having predestinated us unto the adoption of children by Jesus Christ to Himself, according to the good pleasure of His will." One is not so afraid of the word *predestinated* when the sentence begins that way. There is no arbitrariness there, but it is all "in love." Predestination is a manifestation of the love of the Father. As it is God who chose us in grace, it is the Father who has predestinated us to the adoption of children. Nowhere in the Bible are people ever predestinated to go to hell, and nowhere are people simply predestinated to go to heaven. Look it up and see. We are chosen in Christ to share His glory for eternity, but predestination is always to some special place of blessing.

Turn to Romans 8:29: "For whom He did foreknow, He also did predestinate to be conformed to the image of His Son, that He might be the firstborn among many brethren." Predestinated to what? Predestinated "to be conformed to the image of His Son." You see, predestination is not God from eternity saying, "This man goes to heaven and this man to hell." No, but predestination teaches me that when I have believed in Christ, when I have trusted Him as my Saviour, I may know on the authority of God that it is settled forever that some day I am to become exactly like my Saviour. It settles the question of the security of my salvation. Whatever my present unsatisfactory experiences may be, some day I shall be altogether like the One who has redeemed me.

"Having predestinated us unto the adoption of children by Jesus Christ to Himself." That word "adoption" perplexes some. They say, "Does it mean that we are only adopted children and not really born children? A born child is one thing; a child who may not be at all related to the family, but is brought in and adopted, is another. Does it mean adopted in that sense?" This word literally means, the full placing as sons. We might read it, "Having predestinated us unto the son-placing through Jesus Christ unto Himself." It will help us to understand it if we bear in mind that in the days when our Bible was written, ε

man might have a number of wives and some who
were really his slaves. He would have to select
those children among whom he wished to divide
his estate for he might not wish it divided among
this motley company. He would take those whom
he selected down to the forum, and there confess
them openly before the proper authority as his
sons and then go through a ceremony of adoption.
From that day on they were recognized as his
heirs. We have been born into the family of God
by regeneration and thus made children of God.
We have received the Holy Spirit, who is the
Spirit of adoption, and God has marked us out
as those who will share everything with the Son
for all eternity. We are adopted sons and born
again children.

"In love having predestinated us unto the adoption of children by Jesus Christ to Himself,
according to the good pleasure of His will." Our
Lord is the One through whom all this blessing
comes. You know there is a beautiful passage
in the Old Testament which speaks of the coming
Saviour as a "nail in a sure place" (Isa. 22:23).
The simile is taken from the tent-life of the
Arabs. Pegs were fitted into the upright poles
of their dwellings, upon which they hung their
garments and blankets, and upon similar pegs
the women hung the utensils they used. Scripture pictures all kinds of vessels hung on one
of these nails fastened in a sure place, and it

says, "And they shall hang upon him all the glory of his father's house" (Isa. 22:24). So the Lord Jesus Christ having accomplished redemption has become that "nail in a sure place," and every one of us are hung upon Him. If the nail goes down, we all go down; if Christ fails, then we all go down together, but since Christ will never fail, then He will sustain every one of us right on to the very end. That is the truth that is revealed here.

How this truth of election and predestination and of sonship emphasizes the preciousness of our Lord Jesus Christ! Say it over and over to your soul until your whole being is thrilled, "Lord Jesus, I owe it all to Thee." Then you will begin to understand why one enraptured with His love could sing:

> "Jesus, the very thought of Thee
> With sweetness fills my breast;
> But sweeter far Thy face to see,
> And in Thy presence rest."

Every blessing for time and eternity we owe to Him. Is it according to our poor thoughts? Oh, no. According to our apprehensions, according to the strength of our faith, according to our devotedness? Not that. What then? "According to the good pleasure of His will." You know some people are afraid of the will of God, really afraid of it. And yet it is the will of God that you and

I who put our trust in the Lord Jesus should share the Saviour's glory for all eternity; and in revealing His will to us step by step along the way He would have us become more and more conformed to Him down here. Oh, to be able to say from the heart, "I welcome Thy sweet will, O God." The greatest mistake any Christian can make is to substitute his own will for the will of God.

Remember, it is the will of God that every saved one should eventually be with Christ and like Christ forevermore.

> "I know not where His hand shall lead,
>   Through desert wastes, o'er flowery mead;
>   'Mid tangled thicket set with thorn,
>   'Mid gloom of night or glow of morn;
>   But still I know my Father's hand
>   Will bring me to His goodly land."

If you are still unsaved, the most fearful mistake *you* can ever make is to suppose that if you should yield yourself to the will of God it would take away from your peace and happiness and joy. The only real peace, the only real happiness, the only real joy for created beings is found in falling in with the will of God. That will planned our redemption, that will purposed our salvation, and that will secures our place in the glory for all eternity.

ACCEPTED IN THE BELOVED

✦ ✦ ✦

"To the praise of the glory of His grace, wherein He hath made us accepted in the Beloved" (Eph. 1:6).

✦ ✦ ✦

YOU will at once recognize the fact that this verse does not in itself constitute a complete sentence. It is part of a rather lengthy sentence which began with the third verse. We have been climbing one of God's wonderful mountain peaks from that verse, and now we have reached the top. Standing here we are privileged to look below us and see the depths from which we have come, and then look beyond and see the glory that is before us.

There is no room for human boasting. Our salvation is according to the good pleasure of God's will, to the praise of the glory of His own grace, that no man may have opportunity to give himself any credit whatsoever. It is to the praise of the glory of God's grace that He hath made us accepted in the Beloved. I hope we are all clear about grace. We are constantly preaching about it, singing about it, and reading about it, and yet

how few there are who really enter into the
precious fact that our salvation is altogether of
grace. No matter how many times one may
preach on salvation by grace, every time he rises
to face an audience there are scores and possibly
hundreds who are still strangers to the grace of
God. Let us never forget that grace is God's
free unmerited favor lavished upon those who deserve nothing but His judgment. You cannot earn
grace, you cannot earn His loving-kindness.

You may remember the case of the woman who
attempted the assassination of Queen Elizabeth.
She was dressed as a man page, and had secreted
herself in the queen's boudoir awaiting the convenient moment to stab her to death, not realizing
that the queen's attendants would be very careful
to search the rooms before her majesty was permitted to retire. Hidden there among the gowns
they found this woman and brought her into the
presence of the queen. They took from her the
poniard which she had hoped to plant in the heart
of her sovereign. She realized that her case,
humanly speaking, was hopeless, and so she threw
herself down on her knees and pleaded and beg-
ged the queen as a woman, to have compassion
upon her, a woman, her intended assassin, and to
show her grace. Queen Elizabeth looked at her
quietly, and coolly said, "If I show you grace,
what promise will you make for the future?" The
woman looked up and said, "Grace that hath con-

ditions, grace that is fettered by precautions, is no grace at all." Queen Elizabeth caught it in a moment and said, "You are right; I pardon you of my grace," and they led her away a free woman. History tells us that from that moment Queen Elizabeth had no more faithful devoted servant than that woman who had intended to take her life.

Remember grace that hath conditions, grace that is fettered by precautions, that insists upon pledges and promises for the future, is no grace at all. Grace is favor freely shown to those who deserve only judgment, and so we read that our salvation is to the praise of the glory of His grace, and when at last we get home to heaven, He shall have all the praise and all the glory. We will gratefully acknowledge in His blessed presence that left to ourselves we would have gone on to everlasting judgment, that it was He who showed us our deep, deep need. Looking down upon us He pitied us as we were hurrying on to endless woe and He gave His Son to die. This is the grace of our Lord Jesus that led Him to go to Calvary's cross and settle the claim that we never could have settled. And so by grace, and by grace alone, have we been saved.

Observe what grace has done for us: "Wherein He hath made us accepted in the Beloved." There are several other suggested translations of this passage. It might be rendered, "To the

praise of the glory of His grace, which He hath
freely bestowed upon us in the Beloved," or "To
the praise of the glory of His grace wherein He
has taken us into favor in the Beloved."   But all
these different renderings suggest just exactly the
same thing, that the saved sinner does not stand
before God in any righteousness of his own, that
he does not plead any merit of his own before
the divine throne, but that through grace he has
been received to the very heart of God.   Not
merely forgiven, not merely justified, not merely
washed from his sins or cleansed from his defilement, but received in loving-kindness to the very
heart of God according to the Father's estimate
of His own beloved Son.   In the seventeenth chapter of John our blessed Lord speaks to the Father
of His own, of you and of me, if we have believed
in Him, for He was praying for those "who shall
believe on Me through their word."   Thus He
included all believers to the very end of time, and
speaking of such He says to the Father, "That
the world may know that Thou hast loved them,
as Thou hast loved Me."   I could not believe that
if it were not in my Bible; I could not believe
that God, the Holy One, loves me a poor sinner in
myself, a poor sinner who never retires at night
without having to lift my heart to Him in penitence and confess my failures, as He loves the
Lord Jesus Christ, His holy, spotless Son.

We do not have far to go for the proof of His

love. It is seen in that God commended His own love toward us in that He sent His Son to be the propitiation for our sins. If He gave His Son for me, then He must love me as greatly as He loves His Son, or He never would have permitted Him to die for me. And then again, you remember that kindred passage in the fourth chapter of First John, "That we may have boldness in the day of judgment; because as He is, so are we in this world," that is, as He is in relation to judgment. He has already passed through the judgment and will never have to go into it again. He will never again know the forsaking of God, the enshrouding of His soul with the blackness of darkness, the taste of the bitter cup, the agony, shame, and curse of the cross. All that is in the past. He went through it all for us and now so truly are we linked up with Him that, "As He is, so are we in this world."

A very interesting volume has been recently published, giving the story of the life and work of Dr. Usher, who for a great many years carried on medical missionary work in Turkey. In this wonderful story he relates one incident that illustrates in a very striking way what we have before us. He tells how a very notable member of the Turkish movement had become governor of a certain province, in which the mission hospital and schools were located. This man was very learned and of great determination, but a very rigid

Mussulman. He had made up his mind to act in accordance with one of the old laws of Turkey stating that foreigners coming into the country should be allowed to live there for one year, but if at the end of that time they had not become Mohammedans, they would have to leave Turkey. That law had been a dead letter for a great many years, but he made up his mind that he would banish all the missionaries, Catholic and Protestant, from his province.

However, he decided that he would be fair, and he would give them all an opportunity to become Mohammedans, and so during the month of Ramadan, their annual fast, he invited all these missionaries to a great feast in his home. You see, they could feast at night but not in the daytime. As all these missionaries received the message, they knew it to be a summons, for according to Turkish law it would never do to make excuses, for the invitation to dine with the governor was tantamount to a command. Dr. Usher sat on the left hand of the governor, and the Chaldean Catholic bishop sat on his right hand, with the other missionaries on either side, and a number of the attendants of the governor in waiting.

By-and-by, turning to the Catholic bishop, the governor said, "My lord bishop, will you tell me how you think a man can enter paradise?" The bishop answered, "I will say that I believe

through the merits of Jesus Christ, God can forgive my sins and take me to paradise." "Not at
all," said the governor; "I cannot believe that God
is less righteous than I am, and I do not believe
it would be righteous for God because of His
friendship for another, to forgive a sinner and
take him to paradise. If some one here had become indebted to the government and I had to put
him in prison, and some one said, 'That man is a
friend of mine, for my sake I beg you let him go
free,' no matter how much I would desire to
please my friend, I would be an unrighteous governor to let him go free simply because of my
friendship for some one who was interested in
him. I do not believe that God is less righteous
than I." The Chaldean bishop had not another
word to say and sat there looking puzzled. Dr.
Usher felt that something tremendous was at
stake, and he knew that he would be questioned
next, so he lifted his heart to God, remembering
the word, "When they deliver you up, take no
thought how or what ye shall speak: for it shall
be given you in that same hour what ye shall
speak" (Matt. 10:19). He prayed, "Lord, by Thy
Spirit give me now the message." The governor
turned and said, "What would you say? How
may a man be assured of an entrance into paradise?" Dr. Usher replied, "Your Excellency, will
you permit me to use your own illustration, only
to change it slightly? Let us think of you not

merely as the governor of this province, but as the king. You have one son, the prince, whom you love tenderly. Suppose that I am the man who is in debt to the government, owing a sum so vast that I could not pay one part out of a thousand. In accordance with the law, I am laid hold of and cast into prison. Unworthy as I am, your son is a friend of mine: he has a deep interest in me and a real love for me. He seeks you out and says, 'My father, my friend is in prison for a debt which he owes the government, and which he cannot pay. Will you permit me to pay it all for him in order that he may go free?' And you say to him, 'My son, since you are so interested and willing to pay the debt yourself, I am willing that it should be so, and more than that, I will participate with you in it.' And so he goes to the proper authority and pays my debt in full, leaving nothing to be demanded. He takes the receipt, and comes down to me in my prison cell. I could treat him in three ways. When he comes to me and says, 'Brother, your debt is paid and you may go free,' I could turn in haughtiness and say, 'No; I refuse to be under obligation to anybody,' forgetting that my debt is already an obligation and that I am now only entering into one of loving-kindness, whereas I was before obligated by law. Or suppose I say, 'I will never leave this prison unless I can pay the debt myself.' I would have to remain in the prison, for I could not settle the debt. Then, I might look at the receipt and say, 'Yes; but I can't believe it; there is some mistake about it. I can't believe that you would take such an interest in me. I dare not leave; let me remain here. I would be afraid to go out lest the first police officer would arrest me again.' But he might say, 'Man, it is foolish for you to talk like that.' And if he should insist on drawing me out of the prison, I should go slinking down the street and trembling as I thought of my debt, and my home would become a prison for I would be afraid to look out of the window or go to the door. I would have no assurance if I did not believe the message that your son brought. But in the third place I could rise up and fall at the feet of the prince, your son, and say, 'I can never repay you for what you have done for me, but I shall seek to show by my life how grateful I am.' And so I would go free. Let us suppose that on some later day I see the prince riding down one of the streets of the city, and I notice that some one has let a great pile of cord-wood lie in the street which hinders him from going by. Would I try to get some one to get this out of the way? No; but how glad I would be to run out and clear a passage for the prince. If he should say, 'Thank you; let me pay you for your labor,' I would say, 'Oh, no; you paid my debt; it is a joy for me to do something to show my gratitude.' "

The Turkish governor was listening carefully and watching intently, and suddenly a light shone, and he said, "Oh, then, Mr. Usher, is this the reason why you have a hospital here in Turkey? Is this why you establish these schools and why you missionaries are giving your lives for our people? It is not trusting to earn your way into paradise?" "No," said Dr. Usher; "our way into paradise is settled because Jesus has paid the debt, and now we serve because we love Him." The Turkish governor was thoughtful again and then looked up and said, "You used the illustration of my son paying the debt, and you suggested by that that you meant that God has a Son; but God is one God; He does not beget, and He is not begotten. I cannot accept the idea that God should come down to this world and beget a Son." Dr. Usher said, "But, Your Excellency, when God speaks to us He has to use our language. His thoughts are above our thoughts and His words above our words. We speak to one another in different tongues. If I were to say to you in English, 'In a little while I am going home,' it would mean something altogether different from the message which would be conveyed in Turkish, for in Turkish there is no word for home. I would have to say, 'In a little while I am going to the house;' but I do not mean that I am going to the building, I mean that I am going to the love of my wife and children whether there is a building or not. That constitutes home for me. And, you see, our poor human language has no word to express the infinite mystery of the relation between the Father and the Son, for it is not such a relationship as you and I know; it is one that existed from all eternity."

The governor felt he could not banish them, and allowed the work to go on and was himself dismissed from his position because of his grace and kindness in protecting the missionaries. They have always hoped that deep in his heart he turned to Christ.

Our blessed Lord saw us in our deep need. He paid for us, and having settled the debt He has now brought us into the royal family, washed us from every stain of sin, robed us in garments of glory and beauty and given us a seat at the table of the King. He has taken us into favor in the Beloved so that the Father's thoughts of Christ are His thoughts of love for us who trust Christ. Out of this, you see, springs the obedience of faith; out of this springs the earnest desire to so labor, so work, so live for God that in that coming day when we meet our Saviour in the glory, we shall be acceptable to Him and shall hear Him say to us, "Well done, thou good and faithful servant; enter thou into the joy of thy Lord" (Matt. 25:21).

He does not mean that we enter paradise because of our service, but that entering heaven in all the infinite value of the Person and work of Christ we share His joy through the ages to come because of devotion to the One who loves us and gave Himself for us.

REDEMPTION BY HIS BLOOD

✦ ✦ ✦

"In whom we have redemption through His blood, the forgiveness of sins, according to the riches of His grace" (Eph. 1:7).

✦ ✦ ✦

WE have noticed that we were thought of and our happiness planned for by God long before the world began, that when the fulness of time had come, He sent the Lord Jesus Christ into the world to carry out the divine purpose, and that since His death and resurrection, since His ascension to God's right hand in heaven, He has made us accepted in the Beloved. In verse 7 we have the basis of it, "In whom we have redemption." I wish that we might have that firmly fixed in our minds. We do not have to pray, "Take all my guilt away;" we do not have to plead with God to save or to justify us, because these things are blessedly settled and settled for eternity, if we have trusted the Lord Jesus Christ. And so we do not hope some day to receive the redemption of our soul. We have redemption, we have "redemption through His blood, the forgiveness of sins, according to the riches of His grace."

Many of you know that there are three very distinct words used in the New Testament for *redemption*. One of these words means simply to go into the market and buy, "to purchase;" and when you buy a thing, of course it is yours. We have been bought with a price, even the precious blood of the Lord Jesus Christ. We have been redeemed to God by Him and belong to Him. He purchased us, He paid the price for us, made us His own. We sold ourselves for nothing, but we have been redeemed without money, even the precious blood of Christ.

There is another word, a little fuller word, for *redemption,* and this means "to buy out of the market," so that that which has been purchased shall never be put on sale again. For instance, when one went into the slave-market of old and saw a certain slave for sale, and said, "I will purchase this person," when the money was paid the slave was handed over to the purchaser. Then he put into the hand of the slave a legal paper, a writ, which granted him complete freedom—that is the meaning of the second word, "to buy out of the market," never to be placed in jeopardy again. It is the word that is used where Peter tells us we have been redeemed not with "corruptible things, as silver and gold . . . but with the precious blood of Christ, as of a lamb without

blemish and without spot: who verily was foreordained before the foundation of the world, but
was manifest in these last times for you, who by
Him do believe in God, that raised Him up from
the dead, and gave Him glory; that your faith and
hope might be in God" (1 Pet. 1: 18-21). We
have been "bought out of the market," we are not
going to be put on sale any more. We are free.

The third word is the one found in our text. It
is a Greek compound, the first part, *apo,* means
"away from," going away from something or
some condition, and the second part, *lutrosis,*
means "to be free," "to be loosed," and so it means
literally, "to be loosed away" from something. We
have been loosed away from the curse of the law
that once hung over us. We have been loosed
away from the judgment of God toward which we
were one time speeding, loosed away from the
guilt of our sins. That is why I won't sing, "Take
all my guilt away." My guilt was taken away,
for we have been loosed away from the entire
question of guilt. God will never permit that
question to be raised again. It was raised with
His own blessed Son at Calvary's cross when all
the judgment that my guilt deserved fell on Him,
and now I can say:

> "Death and judgment are behind me,
>   Grace and glory are before;
> All the billows rolled o'er Jesus,
>   There exhausted all their power."

Why, it ought to thrill our souls and fill us with
a flood of joy continually. No wonder we sometimes sing:

> "Redeemed, redeemed, from sin and all its woe.
> Redeemed, redeemed, eternal life to know,
> Redeemed, redeemed, by Jesus' blood!
> Redeemed, redeemed! Oh, praise the Lord!"

If we should hold our peace when we realize
what grace hath wrought on our behalf, the very
stones would cry out.

Then notice the price of our redemption—"In
whom we have redemption through His blood."
No less a price would do; no less a price would
have availed to set us free, to deliver us from the
curse and the judgment once hanging over us.
In Old Testament times the sinner came to the
altar bringing a lamb or a goat from the flock,
or a bullock from the herd, or, if very poor, two
turtle-doves, two young pigeons. These were
slain, the blood poured out, and they were offered
upon the altar and consumed by the fire of divine
judgment, a typical sacrifice for sin. But,

> "Not all the blood of beasts
>   On Jewish altars slain,
> Could give the guilty conscience peace
>   Or wash away its stain."

Why? Because there was not sufficient value in
those creatures that were offered up through all
past dispensations. They did not have intrinsic

worth. When that blood was shed and was sprinkled upon the altar and upon the poor sinner, it was powerless to avail, it was powerless to settle the sin question; but, thank God, in our Lord Jesus Christ we see a sacrifice of infinite worth.

People try to reason sometimes as to the extent of His atonement. Some theologians have talked about a limited atonement, for they believe that our blessed Lord made an atonement for a certain elect company only, and that outside of that company there is no possibility of salvation for anyone. Let me say this soberly, seriously, and knowing in my very soul that I have the backing of the Word of God—If every sinner who has ever lived in the world and every sinner who will ever live were to come to God in faith owning his sin and guilt and putting his trust in the Lord Jesus Christ, so infinite is the value of the work of the cross, of the life that was there given, of the precious blood that was there shed, that every sinner could be redeemed from judgment, be freed from every charge, and still there would be untold value in the atonement of Christ which would avail for the sinners in a million universes like this one. There is no measuring the atoning value of the blood of Jesus. I remember hearing a Roman Catholic priest say that one drop of the precious blood of Jesus could wash away all the sins that have ever been committed in this world.

He was right, because, you see, on the one hand, you have finite sinners, and on the other hand, you have the infinite atonement of the Son of God. "We have redemption through His blood." Do you fear then to rest upon this wonderful gospel truth? Do you fear then to trust your soul to the blessed Saviour who there died for your sins on the cross?

Dr. Joseph Parker of London, the noted English preacher, who for many years proclaimed the Word of God in the great City Temple, tells in his autobiography that there was a time when he gave too much attention to the modern theories of his day. Men were reasoning and speculating and undervaluing the Word of God and he found himself, as he read their books and mingled in their meetings, losing his grip intellectually upon the great fundamental doctrine of salvation alone through the atoning blood of the Lord Jesus Christ. But he tells us that there came into his life the most awful sorrow that he ever had to bear. His devoted wife, whom he loved so tenderly, was stricken, and in a few short hours was snatched away from him, He was unable to share his grief with others, and walking through those empty rooms of his home with a breaking heart, his misery felt for some footing in modern theory and there was none, "And then," he said, addressing a company of his Congregational brethren, "my brethren, in those hours of darkness, in those hours of my soul's anguish, when filled with doubt and trembling in fear, I bethought myself of the old gospel of redemption alone through the blood of Christ, the gospel that I had preached in those earlier days, and I put my foot down on that, and, my brethren, I found firm standing. I stand there today, and I shall die resting upon that blessed glorious truth of salvation alone through the precious blood of Christ."

> "On Christ the solid Rock I stand,
> All other ground is sinking sand."

Redemption by blood—in what way does the blood of Christ save us? The blood is the life. The Word of God tells us, "The life of the flesh is in the blood: and I have given it to you upon the altar to make an atonement for your souls" (Lev. 17: 11). Of what blood is He speaking? What blood is given upon the altar to make an atonement? It is the precious blood of Christ, of which all these sacrifices of old were simply typical. Upon the cross God gave Jesus, and there He gave up His life when He poured out His blood. It is through the giving of His life, and not through our imitating the life of Jesus, that we are saved. It is through the outpouring of the life of Jesus in the shedding of His blood that we find redemption. "The Son of God, who loved me, and gave Himself for me" (Gal. 2: 20). And so we have redemption through His blood, and this necessarily involves the forgiveness of sins.

This subject of forgiveness of sins perplexes people sometimes. Forgiveness is presented in Scripture in three very distinct aspects. First, there is eternal forgiveness, and that is what the apostle is speaking of here. Every believer is eternally forgiven the moment he comes to God through Jesus. He stands before God justified, every trespass forgiven and as clear before the throne of God as if he had never committed a sin. He never again has to come to God suing for forgiveness, for He has forgiven all his trespasses. But you may say, "Well, do you mean by that, all my trespasses up to the hour of my conversion?" I mean something far more than that, something far better than that. I mean that the believer's sins, all of them, past, present, and whatever sins may be committed in the future, were all taken into account and were all atoned for when Jesus died, and the moment a man trusts in Him, all the value of that atoning work is put down to his account and every sin is forgiven. That is the first great aspect of forgiveness.

In the second place, there is the restorative forgiveness of the Father. The eternal forgiveness is God's forgiveness—God, the Judge of all. The moment my responsibility for my actions as a sinner ended, that moment my responsibility as a child having to do with my Father began, and if

I fail (and I do, and you do), I come to Him not
to beg forgiveness, for that is settled in the cross,
but I come knowing that, "If we confess our sins
He is faithful and just to forgive us our sins, and
to cleanse us from all unrighteousness." When
as a believer I fail, I come to God as my Father
and tell out the story of my failure and my sin;
and I know on the authority of the Word of God,
that as I confess my sin, it is put away and my
communion with the Father is restored. Sin on
the part of the believer does not affect his life, for
his life is hid with Christ in God, but it does
affect his communion with the Father, and that
is not restored again until the failing believer
comes confessing his sins. Then he receives
restorative forgiveness.

The third aspect has been called "governmental
forgiveness." It has to do with the temporal con-
sequences of sin. I think of a Christian man
whom I have known for a great many years, who
in his unsaved days was an inebriate, giving himself to drunkenness for years. Though that man
lived a wonderful Christian life for over thirty
years, he suffered all his life in his body because
of his early sins. Sometimes he was tempted to
wonder whether God had really forgiven him
when the punishment of sin seemed to be going
on in his body. Again and again you will find
this. God permits temporal punishment to follow
sin, but when the believer learns to take every-

thing as from the hand of God and bows to the
will of God, He sometimes even grants him governmental forgiveness and restores the body, restores the years that the locusts have eaten, and
brings back temporal blessings that one might
have supposed were forever forfeited.

Upon what is all this based? It is "according
to the riches of His grace." It does not say "*out*
of the riches of His grace," but "*according* to the
riches of His grace." Can you estimate the riches
of God's grace? How rich is He in grace? Is He
a millionaire? More than that. Is He is a multi-
millionaire? More than that. Is He a billionaire,
a trillionaire? More than that. Shall I go on?
It is useless, for God's grace is infinite, and you
and I have been blessedly saved, forgiven, redeemed, "according to the riches of His grace."
I repeat, it is not merely *out* of the riches of His
grace. Here is a millionaire to whom you go on
behalf of some worthy cause. He listens to you
and says, "Well, I think I will do a little for you,"
and he takes out his pocketbook and selects a ten-
dollar bill. Perhaps you had hoped to receive a
thousand from him. He has given you *out* of his
riches, but not *according* to his riches. If he gave
you a book of signed blank checks all numbered,
and said, "Take this, fill in what you need," that
would be *according* to his riches.

We who are saved may well rejoice, for we
have been forgiven, we have been redeemed, not

out of the riches of God's grace but *"according* to the riches of His grace." Do you get it? If you do, you will never feel poor again. And you owe it all to the work of the cross, to the blessed One who there died, and through eternity we are going to join with all the redeemed up yonder and ascribe all power and praise and honor and glory to the Lamb that was slain, "who redeemed us to God by Thy blood out of every kindred, and tongue, and people, and nation" (Rev. 5: 9).

May I quote the beautiful words of one of our Christian poets, as emphasizing this precious truth?—

> *"O spotless Lamb, my Sacrifice,*
> *Thou art my soul's salvation;*
> *In God's eternal counsel, Thou,*
> *Before the earth's creation,*
> *Wert slain; our God had planned it all*
> *Ere Satan caused Thy creatures' fall*
> *That shrouded them in darkness.*
> *Naught we could do the gulf to span*
> *'Twixt God and sinful fallen man,*
> *Created in God's likeness.*
>
> *"God saw us in our deep, deep need,*
> *He undertook to save us;*
> *. 'Twas not a trifling thing to Him,*
> *His very best He gave us.*
> *Then mercy's fountain to reveal,*
> *Our weary, sinsick souls to heal,*
> *His Father-heart not sparing,*
> *From Godhead's fullest glory, He*
> *Sent His own Son to earth—I see*
> *Him now my burden bearing.*

"Oh, love of God, how great and strong
  Beyond all human telling!
Oh, wondrous gift!   The Father's Son,
  All doubt and gloom dispelling,
The Lord of glory comes to earth,
A Virgin chosen gave Him birth,
  His bed a lowly manger;
Angels adoring hover near,
Shepherds the great glad tidings hear,
  But to Thine own a stranger.

"In adoration, praise, and love,
  My heart is bowed before Thee;
I trust Thy grace, believe Thy Word.
  It full assurance gives me
That all my sins are washed away
By Thine own blood!   Oh, let me stay
  Close by Thy side forever.
I am Thine own, and Thou art mine!
Who from Thy heart and love sublime,
  And joy and peace, can sever?"

—H. A. M.

THE DISPENSATION OF THE FULNESS OF TIMES

✓ ✓ ✓

"Wherein He hath abounded toward us in all wisdom and prudence; having made known unto us the mystery of His will, according to His good pleasure which He hath purposed in Himself: that in the dispensation of the fulness of times He might gather together in one all things in Christ, both which are in heaven, and which are on earth; even in Him: in whom also we have obtained an inheritance, being predestinated according to the purpose of Him who worketh all things after the counsel of His own will: that we should be to the praise of His glory, who first trusted in Christ. In whom ye also trusted, after that ye heard the word of truth, the gospel of your salvation: in whom also after that ye believed, ye were sealed with that Holy Spirit of promise" (Eph. 1: 8-13).

✓ ✓ ✓

GOD has many counsels but only one purpose, and that purpose is fully brought before us in these verses. In carrying out this purpose He has His counsels in regard to the people of Israel and to the nations of the Gentiles. "In thee shall all the families of the earth be blessed," He said to Abraham. And He has His formerly hidden counsel, now made

known, in regard to the Church which is "the
fulness—the completion—of Him that filleth all
in all." He has His counsels in regard to the
glorious coming kingdom, when our Lord Jesus
shall reign from the river to the ends of the earth.
But all these are but different parts of His one
glorious purpose.

"He hath abounded toward us in all wisdom
and prudence." We may think of this first of all
as the display of His divine wisdom and intelligence; but there is more than that, there is the
subjective side. "He hath abounded *toward us*
in all wisdom and prudence—intelligence." That
is, God, through His Word, through the revelation
of His purpose given to His believing people, to
those who search His Word, believe His Word,
and enter into His truth, gives wisdom and intelligence in divine things which no one else ever
had in all the ages of the past. While there were
unnumbered saints of God in former dispensations, none had the intelligence in divine things
which you and I ought to have.

Even "the angels of His might" never had the
intelligence of His wonderful plan that the weakest Christian may now have if he will. We are
told that angels are learning the wisdom of God
in us. He never gave to them a complete revelation of what was coming; but they are learning
the wisdom, the counsels, the purpose of God, as
they behold His grace displayed in us. The

Church then is an object-lesson to angels. It was given to us to enter into these things, and not merely for intellectual gratification but in order that the truth might build us up in Christ, might form us morally and make us what God would have us be. "And every man that hath this hope set on Him purifieth himself even as He is pure" (1 John 3:3). We are not to view divine mysteries simply as lines of truth upon which to exercise our human intelligence; but we are to be sanctified through the truth. The revelation that God has given should so grip our souls and exercise our consciences that it will lead us to behave as a people who are truly strangers and pilgrims down here, looking for that glorious era which Christ will bring in when He returns.

"He hath abounded toward us in all wisdom and intelligence," as this word, "prudence," really means. "Having made known unto us the mystery of His will." We need to remind ourselves that this word, "mystery," so frequently used in the New Testament, does not necessarily mean something mysterious, something difficult of apprehension, but rather a secret which no one could understand until it was revealed. The mysteries of the kingdom of heaven, the mystery of lawlessness, of Babylon, the great mystery of Christ and the Church, the mystery of the rapture, the mystery of Israel's present rejection, as illustrated in the olive tree of Rom. 11, once hidden secrets which no man could understand, are now opened up to the people of God, and so it is the responsibility of a minister of Christ to expound these mysteries to the saints. We read that such are "stewards of the mysteries of God" (1 Cor. 4:1). From the treasure that God has given them they draw things new and old, and open them up to God's people so that they may enter into the good of them.

What is the mystery of His will? "Having made known unto us the mystery of His will, according to His good pleasure which He hath purposed in Himself: that in the dispensation of the fulness of times He might gather together in one all things in Christ, both which are in heaven, and which are on earth; even in Him." Here, succinctly, clearly, in one brief verse, we have the summing up of the mystery of God. Everything is working on to this one *near-at-hand* "divine event toward which the whole creation moves," when God will head up everything in Christ.

What is meant by a "dispensation?" The word, "dispensation," is used a number of times in the English New Testament, and other words are also used to translate the same Greek word, sometimes "stewardship," "order," "administration," and here "dispensation." We find that the original word has been brought right over into English; it is our word "economy." "That in the economy of the fulness of times He might head up everything in Christ." What is an economy? An economy is an ordered condition of things. Domestic economy is the ordering of a house. But the economy of one house is not necessarily the economy of every other house. If Christians would only bear that in mind, it would save a great deal of confusion. Then there is political economy. The ordering of the affairs of one nation is not the economy of another. The economy of Soviet Russia is not, and I hope will never be, that of the United States of America; the economy of Fascist Italy is not the economy of Democratic England. These nations have their own ways of ordering their affairs, and if one came from Soviet Russia to the United States and attempted to order his conduct according to the economy of Russia, it would not be tolerated here. It might be lawful and right there, but not here. And so there are these various economies running through the Word of God. A dispensation, an economy, then, is that particular order or condition of things prevailing in one special age which does not necessarily prevail in another.

There is a difference between a dispensation and an age. An age is a period of time in which a particular economy prevails. There was the economy before the flood when God was dealing with men according to conscience. We do not know just how God's children met and carried on a public testimony in those days. All that we have concerning that particular time is given us in two or three brief chapters. But after the flood, there was a new economy; civil magistracy was instituted by God for the restraint of human conduct. Then we see God calling Abraham out, and making him to be the beginning of a new race of people to whom He entrusted a new economy, the promise of the coming Seed through whom all nations of the earth should be blessed. And then at Mount Sinai the law was given to the people of Israel. That economy was in force until our blessed Lord cried, "It is finished," on Calvary's cross. Now in the present age of the grace of God, we have this wonderful dispensation of the Holy Spirit, in which the gospel of God is being sent out into all the world. There is no one favored nation, but God's grace goes out to all nations. We are not under law as a principle either of salvation or of life, but we are under grace, saved by Christ, kept by Christ, called upon to walk in Christ to the praise of the glory of His grace. By-and-by there will be another glorious economy, "The dispensation of the fulness of times." That will be in the last glorious age, which has been called ever since the dawn of the Christian era, "The Millennium," "The Reign of Righteousness," when,

> "Jesus shall reign where'er the sun,
> Does his successive journeys run;
> His kingdom spread from shore to shore,
> Till moons shall wax and wane no more."

It is not a dispensation of blessing merely for this world, but heaven and earth will be brought into wonderful unity, and heavenly saints and earthly saints will find their headship in Christ.

"That in the dispensation of the fulness of times He might gather together in one all things in Christ, both which are in heaven, and which are on earth; even in Him." How important then that we know something about what God is doing, that we understand intelligently our dispensational place in the ways of God. Into what confusion of mind many Christians have fallen because, though they are living in this age and are under our special dispensation, they are trying to behave according to another dispensation, confusing law with grace.

How many Christians need to understand these distinctions! They are in confusion of mind all their lives because they do not see the difference between God's order for the house of Israel of old, and for the house of God, the Church, which is the "pillar and ground of the truth," in this present age, to be succeeded by the glorious dispensation of the fulness of times yet to come in what we generally call the Millennium. St. Augustine said, "Distinguish the ages, and the Scriptures are plain."

So God has revealed to us His purpose of grace. He has opened up the good pleasure of His will that we might understand what His plan is for

Israel, the Church, and the world. What a wonderful time it will be when everything unchristian will be put down, when the authority of the Lord Jesus Christ will be owned not only by all in heaven but by all on earth. This is the time referred to in Colossians 1:20: "Having made peace through the blood of His cross, by Him to reconcile all things unto Himself; by Him, I say, whether they be things in earth, or things in heaven." Notice there are only two spheres when Scripture speaks of the future reconciliation. It never includes the sad, unhappy abode of the lost; it simply says that all things in heaven and all things in earth are some day to be reconciled to God through Jesus Christ. But Scripture also speaks of the subjugation of all things, of how God is going to subdue all things to Christ, "That at the name of Jesus every knee should bow, of things in heaven, and things in earth, and things under the earth." All created intelligences will own the authority of our Lord Jesus Christ, but all in heaven and all on earth are to be reconciled to Him in the dispensation of the fulness of times, when He will "gather together in one all things in Christ, both which are in heaven, and which are on earth; even in Him."

And when the apostle, speaking as a Jew by nature, as one who belongs to the people to whom the message first came, says, "In whom also we have obtained an inheritance, being predestinated

—being marked out beforehand—according to the purpose of Him who worketh all things after the counsel of His own will: that we should be to the praise of His glory, who first trusted in Christ," literally, "who pre-trusted in Christ." God has made wonderful promises to Israel, to be fulfilled when "they shall see the King in His beauty," and shall cry, "This is our God; we have waited for Him." Israel in that day will be born again and will turn to the Lord. But Paul himself, an Israelite, says, "We (he and his companions) have already trusted in Christ — we have pre-trusted in Him before this day of His glorious revelation."

"In whom ye (Gentiles) also trusted, after that ye heard the word of truth, the gospel of your salvation: in whom also after that ye believed, ye were sealed with that Holy Spirit of promise." You see, first those of the kindred according to the flesh, and then those of the nations who were alienated and enemies from God by wicked works.

Notice that the greatest objective then for all Christians is that which so many of God's beloved people sometimes neglect, it is the truth of the coming again of our Lord Jesus Christ. The Church's complete blessing awaits His coming, every individual's blessing awaits His coming, the redemption of our bodies awaits His coming, the conversion of Israel awaits His coming, and the full redemption of all the Gentile peoples awaits the coming of our blessed Saviour. How we should long for this great event, watch for it as one watches for the morning. Frances Havergal has expressed the Christian's attitude in a beautiful way:

> "Thou art coming, O our Saviour!
>   Coming, God's anointed King!
> Every tongue Thy Name confessing,
>   Well may we rejoice and sing.
> Thou art coming! Rays of glory
>   Through the veil Thy death has rent,
> Gladden now our pilgrim pathway,
>   Glory from Thy presence sent.
>
> "Thou art coming! Thou art coming!
>   We shall meet Thee on Thy way;
> Thou art coming! We shall see Thee,
>   And be like Thee on that day.
> Thou art coming! Thou art coming!
>   Jesus, our beloved Lord;
> Oh, the joy to see Thee reigning,
>   Worshipped, glorified, adored!
>
> "Thou art coming! Not a shadow,
>   Not a mist, and not a tear,
> Not a sin, and not a sorrow,
>   On that sunrise grand and clear.
> Thou art coming! Blessed Saviour,
>   Nothing else seems worth a thought:
> Oh, how marvelous the glory,
>   And the bliss Thy pain hath bought.
>
> "Thou art coming! We are waiting
>   With a 'hope' that cannot fail,
> Asking not the day or hour,
>   Anchored safe within the veil.

> Thou art coming!   At Thy table
>   We are witnesses of this,
> As we meet Thee in communion,
>   Earnest of our coming bliss."

May it be ours to enter more and more fully, by reverent, prayerful study of and meditation upon the Word of God, into the apprehension of the glorious purpose of His grace that we may walk *now* in the light of that coming dispensation when Christ shall see of the travail of His soul and shall be satisfied!

SEALED WITH THE HOLY SPIRIT

✟ ✟ ✟

"In whom ye also trusted, after that ye heard the word
of truth, the gospel of your salvation: in whom also after that
ye believed, ye were sealed with that Holy Spirit of promise,
which is the earnest of our inheritance until the redemption
of the purchased possession, unto the praise of His glory"
(Eph. 1: 13, 14, R. V.).

✟ ✟ ✟

YOU will notice that these verses carry us
back in thought to what has immediately
preceded in verse 12. There the Apostle
Paul says, "That we should be to the praise of
His glory, who first trusted in Christ," and he
speaks as a representative believer from Israel.
The gospel of God was to the Jew first. Those
who received the message on the day of Pentecost
were all of Israel, although they came from the
many different parts of the world into which
they had been scattered because of their sins.
Wherever the message went it was to the Jew first
in those early days, and the Apostle Paul, himself
a Jew, could speak of the glorious privileges
which belonged to them who had become the
people of God in Christ.

In verse 13 he turns to the Gentile converts; therefore the words are especially appropriate as applied to ourselves, "In whom ye also trusted." Notice the different pronoun. It is "ye," Gentiles. "In whom ye also trusted, after that ye heard the word of truth." He does not necessarily imply any lengthy period after they had heard the word of truth. It might be rendered, "In whom ye also trusted, upon hearing the word of truth." The gospel message believed results in immediate salvation. It is not necessary that people go through a long season of soul-exercise and travail of spirit after hearing the gospel before they are converted to God. A man may hear the message for the first time, and hearing, believe and live. Yet one can quite understand the pitiful question of the Chinese woman who had lived in the darkness of paganism all her life. Some itinerant missionaries came to her village, and for the first time, she feared the only time, she heard the message of grace. She came trembling and said, "It is a wonderful story. I have never heard it before, and you are leaving us tomorrow. I may never hear it again, but I believe it. Do you think once is enough to make my soul secure?" Yes, once is enough!

> "Once for all, O sinner, receive it,
> Once for all, O brother, believe it:
> Cling to the cross, the burden will fall,
> Christ hath redeemed us once for all."

Most of us have heard it over and over again. I wonder how many can take these words to ourselves, "In whom ye also trusted, after that ye heard the word of truth, the gospel of your salvation." The gospel is indeed the "good spell." That is the exact meaning of the Anglo-Saxon word, "gospel." Some of the words that we think of as slang are really ground deep in our language. We speak of a soap-box orator as a "spellbinder," and think of that as slang, but the fact is, the word "spell" was used in that way centuries ago. The gospel is the good spell, the good message, God's good news for poor lost sinners; it is God's good news about His blessed Son. It cannot be too often emphasized that the gospel is not good advice to be obeyed; it is good news to be believed. It is something that God has told us about the Lord Jesus Christ, and when we believe the message, we are saved. Now, following our salvation, we are sealed with the Holy Spirit—"In whom also after that ye believed, ye were sealed with that Holy Spirit of promise." A good many have been misled by the rendering here given. "In whom also after that ye believed—" they have thought that this necessarily implied an interval between believing and being sealed with the Spirit; but I would call your attention to the fact that we have exactly the same words as in the previous part of the verse: "In whom ye also trusted, after that ye heard the word of truth."

Not necessarily a week or a month, or yet ten minutes after, but *upon hearing*. And so we read in the latter part of the verse that *upon believing* we were sealed with the Holy Spirit.

There is, of course, a difference between the Holy Spirit's regenerating work and the sealing. The difference is as great as that between building a house and moving into it. You may move into it the moment it is ready. When the Spirit of God creates a man anew in Christ Jesus, that moment a house is built, a temple is prepared, and then the blessed Holy Spirit of God moves in and takes possession of him. "Ye were sealed with that Holy Spirit of promise." That is, the Spirit who had been promised in past ages and by our blessed Lord when here on earth, has now come to indwell every believer. Three times in the New Testament we read of the believer being sealed with the Spirit. We find it here, and in 2 Cor. 1: 22, "Who hath also sealed us, and given the earnest of the Spirit in our hearts," and then in our same epistle (chap. 4: 30), "Grieve not the Holy Spirit of God, whereby ye are sealed unto the day of redemption." These are the only three direct references to the sealing of the Holy Spirit in connection with the believer, but in John 6: 27 we read of the blessed Lord Himself that He was sealed. "Labor not for the meat which perisheth, but for that meat which endureth unto everlasting life, which the Son of Man shall give unto you:

for Him hath God the Father sealed." You remember when He came forth from His baptism in the Jordan, the Spirit of God descended like a dove and abode upon Him, and a voice from heaven said, "This is My beloved Son, in whom I am well pleased" (Matt. 3:17). That is the sealing of the blessed Saviour. It is always interesting to note that it is in the sixth chapter of John's Gospel, where He dwells upon the fact that He is the Living Bread which came down from heaven, which if a man eat he shall live forever, that our Lord speaks of Himself as sealed.

A seal was a stamp, a mark of ownership, a mark of approval. You go to the grocery store and get a loaf of bread, and it has a little stamp on it, or perhaps it has the name of the bakery or the trade mark impressed upon the bread. This was done by pressing the dough into the pan which had the name in the metal. That name upon the loaf of bread is the maker's guarantee. It is as though he says, "I stand back of this bread." It is just so with our blessed Lord. He is the Bread of God, the Living Bread, the Bread of Life, and God the Father sealed Him when He gave Him the Holy Spirit without measure. And now when we believe in Him, trust Him as our Saviour, the same blessed Holy Spirit comes to live in us. God the Father seals us by the Spirit, and says, as it were, "This man, this woman, belongs to Me; henceforth I stand back of him, I own him as Mine."

It is a remarkable thing that the only two epistles in which we read of sealing by the Spirit are Corinthians and Ephesians. Corinth and Ephesus were great centers of the lumber industry in ancient times. A raft of logs would be brought from the Black Sea and notice sent to the different lumber firms that the raft was in the harbor. These firms would send their men out and they would look over the logs and make their selection. One would say, "I will take those logs," another, "I will take these," and they would pay down a little earnest money and then cut a certain wedge upon each log that the firm had agreed to take. This was called the seal. The logs might not be drawn out of the water for many weeks, but each was sealed by the mark of the firm that had undertaken to purchase them. I was standing on a high bridge at St. Cloud, Minn., watching a lumber jam, and as I saw the men working I said to my friend, "Do all these logs belong to one firm?" "Oh, no," he said; "there are representatives of many different firms working here in the Minnesota woods." "Well," I asked, "how on earth can they distinguish between the logs?" He showed me from the bridge how they were marked, so that when they reached their destination down the river, the various firms would be able to select their own logs. Though you and I are still tossing about on the waters of this poor scene we have been sealed by the Holy Spirit of promise, and when the appointed day cames and the blessed Lord takes His own to be with Himself, that will be the day of the redemption of His purchased possession, and He will take out of this world all who have been sealed with His Spirit. We will go to be with Him in yonder bright glory.

We may well remember the word, "Grieve not the Holy Spirit of God, whereby ye are sealed." He who has come to dwell within us will abide with us forever. When the Spirit of God once takes up His abode in a believer, He never leaves him in life or in death, until presented faultless in the presence of the glory of our Lord Jesus Christ. The bodies of our beloved dead in Christ are in the keeping of the Holy Spirit, and living saints are indwelt by the Spirit and will be until called hence to be forever with the Lord.

This enables us to understand the transition of thought as we pass to verse 14. In verse 13 the Holy Spirit is a seal, and in verse 14 He is the earnest, "Which is the earnest of our inheritance until the redemption of the purchased possession, unto the praise of His glory." I mentioned the lumber-dealer paying down a small sum as an earnest, the rest to be paid in full when the logs were drawn out of the water. Our blessed God has given us the Holy Spirit as the earnest, the pledge, that eventually we are to be taken out of this scene and fully conformed to the image of

His Son. Now we are privileged to appropriate in a small measure what we shall have in all its fulness when we get home to heaven. Everything of Christ which we enjoy at all, we enter into by the Holy Spirit.

> "If here on earth the thoughts of Jesus' love
> Lift our poor hearts this weary world above,
> If even here the taste of heavenly springs
> So cheers the spirit, that the pilgrim sings,
>
> "What will the sunshine of His glory prove?
> What the unmingled fulness of His love?
> What hallelujahs will His presence raise?
> What but one loud eternal burst of praise?"

What will it mean when we see Him face to face, when the last vestige of sin and infirmity will disappear, and we shall be like Him for whom we wait? We shall be to "the praise of His glory." Think of it! Every saint of God, every redeemed one, every sinner saved by grace divine, will add to the glory, to the satisfaction of the heart of God throughout eternity. It was in order that we might thus be won for Christ, that we might be set apart for Himself, that our blessed Lord came in grace from the throne in heaven down to the cross of Calvary. It was that He might redeem us to God with His own blood and make us suited habitations for the Holy Spirit's indwelling, that He saved us and made us His own.

PAUL'S FIRST PRAYER FOR THE SAINTS

✓ ✓ ✓

"Wherefore I also, after I heard of your faith in the Lord Jesus, and love unto all the saints, cease not to give thanks for you, making mention of you in my prayers; that the God of our Lord Jesus Christ, the Father of glory, may give unto you the spirit of wisdom and revelation in the knowledge of Him; the eyes of your understanding being enlightened; that ye may know what is the hope of His calling, and what the riches of the glory of His inheritance in the saints, and what is the exceeding greatness of His power to us-ward who believe, according to the working of His mighty power, which He wrought in Christ, when He raised Him from the dead, and set Him at His own right hand in the heavenly places, far above all principality, and power, and might, and dominion, and every name that is named, not only in this world, but also in that which is to come: and hath put all things under His feet, and gave Him to be the Head over all things to the Church, which is His body, the fulness of Him that filleth all in all" (Eph. 1: 15-23).

✓ ✓ ✓

WE have in this letter two prayers offered by the Apostle Paul, not only for the Ephesians but for all the people of God. The first is our present passage and the second is found in chapter three. Notice that he says, "I also, after I heard of your faith in the

Lord Jesus, and love unto all the saints, cease not to give thanks for you, making mention of you in my prayers." He offers his petition for those who are already saved. When people are born of God, one of the first evidences that they possess a new nature is that they feel a sense of dependence upon the Lord and begin to pray, first for themselves, and then their hearts go out in intercession for others. When the Lord sent Ananias to Saul of Tarsus, he objected, saying, "Lord, I have heard by many of this man, how much evil he hath done to Thy saints at Jerusalem, and here he hath authority from the chief priests to bind all that call on Thy name." But the Lord replied, "Behold, he prayeth." This was an evidence of a real work begun in the soul of the erstwhile persecutor of the Church of God, and so Ananias went to him in confidence and laid his hands upon him, saying, "Brother Saul, the Lord, even Jesus, that appeared unto thee in the way as thou camest, hath sent me, that thou mightest receive thy sight, and be filled with the Holy Ghost," and he commanded him to be baptized. It is as natural for the renewed man to pray as it is for the natural man to breathe.

Note how the apostle tells the saints of his confidence in them. He had heard with joy of the way they had been growing in grace, of their faith in the Lord Jesus and love unto all the saints. Where faith is genuine, it will always be manifested by love; not merely to our own peculiar group, but love unto all the saints. This term "saints" is an all-inclusive one, taking in every individual who has been born into the family of God. Some have an idea that all the saints are in heaven, but we do not need to pray for those who are in the presence of the Lord over yonder. Believers on earth are called saints, and for them we need to make intercession.

Paul prays for three distinct things, but first he asks, "That the God of our Lord Jesus Christ, the Father of glory, may give unto you the spirit of wisdom and revelation in the knowledge of Him." Earlier in the chapter, we have already seen how in verse 3 he exclaims, "Blessed be the God and Father of our Lord Jesus Christ." Because the Eternal Son became Man for our redemption, it is right to speak of the God of our Lord Jesus Christ. Because His relationship is ever that of Son, it is equally right to speak of God as His Father. This first prayer is addressed to "the God of our Lord Jesus Christ." When we come to consider the second prayer we shall find that it is addressed to the Father. When we think of God as such, we think of Him as Creator, the Source of all counsel and wisdom ("God is light"), and we notice that in this particular prayer the apostle is especially occupied with the counsels or purpose of God. The other is addressed to the Father because it has to do with the family relationship. "God is love" as well as light.

It is very remarkable how exactly divine titles are used in Holy Scripture. He prays, "That the God of our Lord Jesus Christ, the Father of glory" (or excellence)—all glory proceeds from Him, and glory is but the manifestation of divine excellence—"may give unto you the spirit of wisdom and revelation in the knowledge of Him." He does not mean that you must receive the Holy Spirit in some new and second way. If a Christian, you have the Holy Spirit dwelling in you, but He who indwells you delights in His special work of opening up the things of Christ and revealing them to His saints. How does He do that? By giving insight into the truth already revealed in the Word of God. All Scripture is divinely inspired. Holy men of God spake as they were moved by the Holy Spirit, but the merely natural man reads the Word and sees nothing in it, because he is not acquainted with its Author. The believer who is indwelt by the Holy Spirit reads, and in reading hears the voice of God. So there is all the difference in the world between reading this Book in a cold intellectual way and reading it in the presence of God, depending upon His blessed Holy Spirit to open up its truth to heart and mind. It is then that He acts as the Spirit of wisdom and revelation, giving the believer to enjoy precious things never seen before.

Have you not often heard some servant of God expounding the Word in such a way that it came home to your heart in wondrous power and blessing? Perhaps you said, "It is strange; I have read that passage over and over again, and yet I never saw it like that before. I do not understand how it is that when I read the Bible myself I fail to appreciate these things." Often the real trouble is we do not spend enough time in the presence of God, looking to Him to open up His truth to us.

I remember years ago, while my dear mother was still living, I went home to visit the family, and found there a man of God from the north of Ireland. I was a young Christian at the time, engaged in gospel work. He was a much older man, an invalid, dying of what we then called "quick consumption." He had come out to Southern California, hoping climatic conditions would be of some help to him. But it was evident that he was too far gone to be recovered to health again. He lived, by his own desire, in a small tent out under the olive trees a short distance away from our home. I went out to see him there. I can remember how my heart was touched as I looked down upon his thin worn face upon which I could see the peace of Heaven clearly manifested. His name was Andrew Fraser. He could barely speak above a whisper, for his lungs were almost gone, but I can recall yet how, after

a few words of introduction, he said to me,
"Young man, you are trying to preach Christ;
are you not?" I replied, "Yes, I am." "Well,"
he whispered, "sit down a little, and let us talk
together about the Word of God." He opened
his well-worn Bible, and until his strength was
gone, simply, sweetly, and earnestly he opened up
truth after truth as he turned from one passage
to another, in a way that my own spirit had never
entered into them. Before I realized it, tears
were running down my face, and I asked, "Where
did you get these things? Could you tell me
where I could find a book that would open them
up to me? Did you learn these things in some
seminary or college?" I shall never forget his
answer. "My dear young man, I learned these
things on my knees on the mud floor of a little
sod cottage in the north of Ireland. There with
my open Bible before me, I used to kneel for
hours at a time, and ask the Spirit of God to reveal Christ to my soul and to open the Word to
my heart, and He taught me more on my knees
on that mud floor than I ever could have learned
in all the seminaries or colleges in the world." It
was not many weeks after this that he was absent
from the body and present with the Lord, but the
memory of that visit has always remained with
me and is a most precious recollection. Is it not
true that most of us do not stay long enough in
the presence of God? We do not get quiet enough

to let Him talk to us and reveal His mind to us.

"Meditation," someone has said, "is becoming a lost art in our day." To meditate is really to chew the cud. Just as the cattle take their food in the rough and then ruminate and get the sweetness and the good out of it, so the believer needs to read the Word and then spend time quietly in the presence of God, going over it again and again, ruminating, chewing the cud, until it becomes truly precious to his heart. Of old the Israelites were forbidden to eat the flesh of any animal that did not chew the cud and part the hoof. The parted hoof is a foot that rises above the filth of this world. It has been well said that it is a great thing when the mouth and the foot agree, when we feed on the Word and walk in the power of the truth. It is when one thus gets into the presence of God that the Holy Spirit delights to take of divine things and show them unto us. It is thus we grow in the knowledge of Christ. That is one reason why the Spirit came. Every believer to a certain extent has the knowledge of Christ, but the original word implies more than that. It is not merely knowledge as such; it is really super-knowledge, or full knowledge. "That the God of our Lord Jesus Christ, the Father of glory, may give you the Spirit of wisdom and revelation in the full knowledge of Him." Perhaps you know Him as your Saviour, as the One who has redeemed you from everlasting destruction,

as the glorious Head of the Church, with whom
you are linked by the Holy Spirit. He would
have you go on to know Him better, for there are
riches in Christ that you may be sure you have
never yet entered into. We cannot afford to be
negligent, or to let other things crowd out the
blessing we might have by giving more time to
the teaching of the Holy Spirit.

> "Oh, the pure delight of a single hour
>   That before Thy throne I spend,
>   As I kneel in prayer, and with Thee, my Lord,
>   I commune as friend with friend."

We sing these words sometimes and sing them
rather glibly, but how much do we know of the
reality of spending an hour in His presence,
learning more of Him as the Spirit of God un-
folds precious things that otherwise our hearts
would never enter into?

We have already remarked that there are three
distinct petitions in this prayer. He asks,

1. "That the eyes of your heart being enlightened, ye may know what is the hope of His
   calling."
2. "And what the riches of the glory of His
   inheritance in the saints."
3. "And what is the exceeding greatness of
   His power to us-ward who believe, according to the working of His mighty power."

Notice, it is "That the eyes of your heart being
enlightened." Our Authorized Version reads,

"The eyes of your understanding," but it is not merely the intellect he has in view, it is the heart. Christians understand with the heart. It is "with the heart man believeth unto righteousness." It is with the heart that we enter into divine realities. One may be very brilliant intellectually, but that does not guarantee for a moment that he will have an understanding of spiritual things. It is only as the heart is exercised before God, as the eyes of the heart are opened, that spiritual things will be discerned. That is one reason why people must be born again, otherwise they cannot understand the things of God.

Perhaps an illustration will help to make clear what I mean. Some people are born into the world with a remarkable musical sense, and some have none at all. Now a man who has no sense of tone cannot become a musician, no matter how others may seek to instruct him. Such an one might go to listen to the most wonderful oratorio, but it would all be meaningless to him if he had no appreciation of music. He would really have to be born again, as it were, in order to appraise it aright, and so in regard to spiritual things, one must have a new nature if he would enter into them appreciatively.

But if the eyes of the heart are opened, then one may understand something of "the hope of His calling." Do you understand "what is the hope of His calling?" It is that to which we have

already had our attention drawn in the earlier
part of the chapter: "He hath blessed us with
all spiritual blessings in heavenly places in
Christ; according as He hath chosen us in Him
before the foundation of the world," that we
should be holy and without blame before Him.
This is the hope of His calling; that some day we
shall see Him as He is and be like Him. Our God
has chosen us for this, and He is never going to
give up until we attain to the full stature of men
and women in Christ Jesus.

Then, in the second place, that we may apprehend the riches of the glory of His inheritance in
the saints. Earlier in the chapter we read of the
riches of His grace; here we have the riches of
His glory. We are enjoying the riches of His
grace now and we shall enter into and enjoy the
riches of His glory by-and-by. Notice this expression, "The riches of the glory of His inheritance in the saints." What does that mean? It
does not mean that the saints are His inheritance,
as some would have us believe, but it does mean
that when He takes possession of His inheritance,
He is going to take possession of it through His
saints. It is not our inheritance in Him, observe,
but His inheritance in us. Of old the land of
Canaan was His inheritance, but He took possession of it through His people Israel. By-and-
by He will take possession of a redeemed universe
through His saints and we shall reign with Him.

Who can apprehend our part in that glory? What
will it be when we are with Him and like Him
when He returns to reign, and we shall sit with
Him upon His throne and God will take possession of His inheritance in His saints!

Then observe the third petition: "What is the
exceeding greatness of His power to us-ward who
believe, according to the working of His mighty
power." You see, Christians are not storage bat-
teries. How often we hear people praying, "O
God, give me more power," and you would think
that we were a little bit like these ever-ready
flashlights that you can open up and put a battery
in, then press a button and get a light. You
would imagine that as Christians, the Lord puts
a power battery into us, presses a button, and
then we shine for Him. Nothing of the kind! We
have power only as we are living in fellowship
with Him who is the Source of all power, and as
we are walking in fellowship with Him, the same
power works in and through us that wrought in
Christ when God raised Him from the dead. That
was the fullest manifestation of divine power the
world has ever known.

Our attention is not called to the power that
created the heaven and the earth, to the power
that brought the people of Israel out of Egypt,
parted the Red Sea, and led them in triumph to
the Land of Canaan, nor to the working of mighty
miracles through the Lord and His apostles, but

to the greatest manifestation of the power of God of which we know anything, the resurrection of the Lord Jesus Christ. This is the same power that works in believers who walk in fellowship with Him: "According to the mighty power which He wrought in Christ when He raised Him from the dead and set Him at His own right hand in the heavenly places, far above all principality, and power, and might, and lordship, and every name that is named, not only in this world, but also in that which is to come." By these expressions, "principality," "power," "might," "dominion," we are to understand the countless hosts of angelic beings, glorious sinless spirits serving our blessed Lord, and also serried ranks of evil angels opposed to God and His Christ.

Our Lord went down into the depths, into the grave, descended into the lower parts of the earth, and Satan and his hosts rejoiced when they saw Him under the power of death. But God has raised Him from the dead and taken Him up to His right hand in the highest glory, where as Man He sits today enthroned. The wonderful thing that the apostle dwells on here is that the power that did all that for the Lord Jesus is the power that works in us as believers if we do not hinder it by our frivolity and worldliness. Do not, I beg of you, ever complain again that you have no power to meet temptation, that you have no power to rise above some sinful habit. If you find yourself in that condition it is because you are out of fellowship with God. Get right with Him. Judge the sin that has hindered communion and then, as when you make the electrical connection the power flows through the wire to operate the mighty machinery, so you will be in living touch with God, and divine power will work in and through you to enable you to triumph over sin and live to His glory.

We are told that Christ has gone up "above all principality, and power, and might, and dominion, and every name that is named, not only in this world, but also in that which is to come." And then we are told that He has put all things under His feet. We do not yet see everything subject to Him, but we do see Him seated in the heavenlies above all things, as evidence that all shall eventually acknowledge His rightful sway. Then we have an added word which was never revealed in Old Testament times but is now made known in this dispensation of grace: "And gave Him to be Head over all things to the Church which is His Body, the fulness of Him that filleth all in all." A head without a body is incomplete. The marvelous thing is that the Church is the completeness of Christ; during all this present age He is manifesting Himself through the Church to the world. Some day the members of the Body will be with the Head in the glory, and the one new man will be manifested in all his perfection. Is

it not a wonderful thing then to realize this: that
our blessed Lord would in this sense be incomplete without us? Think of it! We were poor
lost sinners of the Gentiles, deserving nothing but
the judgment of God, but now through His grace
we have been saved, and not only that but made
members of His Body, the Body of Christ, the
completeness of Him that filleth all in all. What
a hallowed responsibility this puts upon us to represent Him aright in this world; to manifest His
grace, His holiness, His love, His hatred of sin,
His compassion for the lost, His desperate earnestness in seeking to reach lost men and make
known to them the riches of His grace. We are
left here to carry on His work in the scene where
He was crucified. May God give us to rise to a
proper sense of our hallowed responsibility and
thus to make Him known as we should.

THE CHRISTIAN'S PAST, PRESENT AND FUTURE

✦ ✦ ✦

"And you hath He quickened, who were dead in trespasses and sins; wherein in time past ye walked according
to the course of this world, according to the prince of the
power of the air, the spirit that now worketh in the children
of disobedience: among whom also we all had our conversation in times past in the lusts of our flesh, fulfilling the desires of the flesh and of the mind; and were by nature the
children of wrath, even as others. But God, who is rich in
mercy, for His great love wherewith He loved us, even
when we were dead in sins, hath quickened us together with
Christ (by grace ye are saved); and hath raised us up
together, and made us sit together in heavenly places in
Christ Jesus: that in the ages to come He might show the
exceeding riches of His grace in His kindness toward us
through Christ Jesus" (Eph. 2: 1-7).

WHILE holding meetings in Southern California I took the inter-urban car one
Saturday to go from Los Angeles to a
well-known beach resort. We had hardly left the
city when a rather peculiar-looking lady (I suppose she was a lady; at any rate, she was of the
feminine persuasion), attired in a strange garb
that made her look as though she was dressed up
in red bandanna handkerchiefs pieced together,

and who wore a shawl on her head with a lot of spangles over her forehead, came and sat down beside me, and said, "How do you do, gentleman? You like to have your fortune told?" I said, "Are you able to tell my fortune?" She held out a winsome little palm and said, "Cross my palm with a silver quarter, and I will give you your past, present, and future." "You are very sure you can do that if I give you a quarter?" I said. "You see, I am Scotch, and should hate to part with a quarter and not get proper exchange for it." She looked bewildered for a moment, but then said very insistently, "Yes, gentleman, I can give you your past, present, and future. I never fail; I have wonderful second sight. Cross my palm with a quarter. Please, gentleman. I will tell you all." I said, "It is really not necessary, because I have had my fortune told already, and I have a little Book in my pocket that gives me my past, present and future." "You have it in a book?" she said. "Yes, and it is absolutely infallible. Let me read it to you," I said, and I pulled out my New Testament. She looked startled when she saw it, but I turned to this second chapter of the Epistle to the Ephesians and said, "Here is my past, 'And you hath He quickened, who were dead in trespasses and sins: wherein in time past ye walked according to the course of this world, according to the prince of the power of the air, the spirit that now worketh in the children of disobedience: among whom also we all had our conversation in times past in the lusts of our flesh, fulfilling the desires of the flesh and of the mind, and were by nature the children of wrath, even as others.'" "Oh, yes," she said; "it is plenty, I do not care to hear more." "But," i said, as I held her gently by the arm, "I want to give you my present also, 'But God, who is rich in mercy, for His great love wherewith He loved us, even when we were dead in sins, hath quickened us together with Christ, (by grace ye are saved;) and hath raised us up together, and made us sit together in heavenly places in Christ Jesus.'" "That is plenty, gentleman," she said; "I do not wish to hear any more." "Oh, but," I replied, "there is more yet, and you must get it; and you are not going to pay me a quarter for it either. I am giving it to you for nothing. It is my past, my present, and my future. Here is the future, 'That in the ages to come He might show the exceeding riches of His grace in His kindness toward us through Christ Jesus.'" She was on her feet, and I could not hold on any tighter lest I should be charged with assault and battery, and she fled down the aisle, saying, "I took the wrong man! I took the wrong man!"

You know how interested people are in trying to delve into the mysterious and unknown. If it were not for this bump of curiosity that so many have, these fortune-tellers and spirit-mediums, who can tell you how to make immense sums of money but are themselves as poor as church mice, would all have to die of starvation. People want to know the things that God has not revealed. But it is amazing to see how indifferent they are to the very important revelation that He has given us in His Word. He has made known the past, the present and the future of the universe, of the nation of Israel, of the great Gentile nations, of the Church of God, and then — what comes home to every Christian—of every individual believer in the Lord Jesus Christ.

"And you hath He quickened." You will notice that the words, "hath He quickened," are in italics. That means that there is nothing in the original to answer to them, and yet we actually seem to need them to fully bring out the thought of the Greek, for in the original the verb comes in the fifth verse, and in order to make it read smoothly in English it is necessary to put in these words. To be quickened is to be made to live. Because we were dead we needed to receive divine life. "You hath He quickened, who were dead in trespasses and sins: wherein in time past ye walked according to the course of this world." What a past! We were utterly beyond any ability to save ourselves, for a dead man can do nothing to improve his condition, and every unsaved person is dead, dead toward God, dead spiritually. If you are out of Christ, you have never had one pulse-beat toward God, you are dead in trespasses and sins. Sin has not only made man guilty so that he needs forgiveness, but sin has sunk the human race into a state of spiritual death so that men need divine life. That is why we must be born again. Being born again is receiving new life from God through faith in the Lord Jesus Christ.

Of course, there are degrees of sinfulness, there are degrees along moral lines. We would not for a moment say everybody is just as corrupt, just as vile, just as wicked, just as despicable, as everybody else. That would not be true; and yet if people are dead, they are dead. The beautiful little maid, the daughter of Jairus, had been dead only a few minutes when the blessed Lord reached her father's house, but she was dead, she was lifeless. Fair to look upon, lovely and sweet, no doubt, in the eyes of her beloved parents, like a beautiful marble statue, but although there was not the corruption that there might have been, she was dead nevertheless. Turn over to Luke's Gospel and you find that as the blessed Lord came to the village of Nain they were carrying a young man out to bury him. He was dead. Dead perhaps a day or two. In the land of Palestine they generally bury the dead either on the day that life ceases or the day immediately following. So this young man was dead longer than the little maid, but life was just as truly extinct in her case as

in his. Then you have the blessed Lord at the
grave of Lazarus. The sisters told Him not to
roll the stone away, for their brother had been
dead four days and would already be offensive.
Corruption had set in, but the Lord Jesus brought
new life to that man. In every instance it took
exactly the same mighty, quickening power to re-
store the dead. Only the Son of God could speak
life to the daughter of Jairus, to the young man
of Nain, and to Lazarus. So we were dead, every
one of us, we who are now saved. Some were
deeply corrupted because of sin, others perhaps
did not know so much of its vileness and corruption, but all alike were dead before God and needed new and divine life.

"Dead in trespasses and sins." Notice the difference between the two expressions. Sinning is
missing the mark. Trespass is the violation of a
definite law. We see the sign, "No trespassing,"
and know that that means that we cannot pass a
certain boundary without being guilty of trans-
gressing. You and I are guilty on both counts.
We are sinners, for we have taken our own way;
and we are trespassers, because we have actually
transgressed what we knew to be the revealed will
of God; and so we are dead to God in our natural
condition. Yet we are able to walk—"Wherein
in time past ye walked according to the course of
this world."

We were dead toward God and could not take

one step with Him. Dr. Gaebelein relates that he was holding meetings in a Y. M. C. A. auditorium, and one day the secretary showed him a card which he was in the habit of passing out. It read, "I promise faithfully henceforth to lead a religious and Christian life," and then there was a place to sign one's name. The secretary said, "How do you like that? Isn't that a pretty good way of putting it?" Dr. Gaebelein said, "How on earth can a dead man live any kind of a life? What is the use of putting a card like that into the hands of a dead sinner, and having him sign it and say, 'I promise faithfully henceforth to lead a religious and Christian life?' You cannot live a life for God until you receive a life from God." You can live according to the world, live a moral life and what some people call a religious life, but that is only "according to the course of this world." For, after all, the world admires morality and religion. If you are a young man looking for a wife, you do not look in the vilest part of the city for some poor wretched characterless girl, you try to find one who has a bit of religion and morality; and a young woman looking for a husband does the same. People have an idea that morality and religion are necessarily Christian. Of course a Christian ought to be characterized by both, but from a much higher motive than the world. The course of this world is often a religious and a moral course, but in independence of Christ.

A little group of Greek philosophers were talking together five hundred years before Christ, and the question was asked, "What is the briefest possible definition of a man?" Plato said, "Man is a two-legged animal." One of them went out, and brought in a rooster. He held him up and said, "Behold Plato's man!" Then one exclaimed, "I have it; man is a religious animal." That is it. There is not another creature in the world but man that ever lifts his eyes toward God and heaven, that ever feels a sense of responsibility to a higher power, and therefore man is incurably religious. Even the atheist is incurably religious. He worships himself, he is his own god. So, we say, the course of this world may be a religious and a moral course. On the other hand, it may be a vile, abominably wicked, sinful course, but it is all the same, it is "the course of this world," and that is the course in which we walked before we were born again.

"According to the prince of the power of the air." He is, of course, the devil. When living in our sins, the devil was our master and we were led by his will.

"The spirit that now worketh in the children of disobedience (those who refuse obedience to God); among whom also we all had our conversation (our manner of living, our desire) in times past in the lusts of our flesh, fulfilling the desires of the flesh and of the mind." We sometimes

think of the word "lust" as though it referred
only to one degrading kind of sin, but it is unlaw-
ful desire of any kind. There are just as truly
lusts of the mind as lusts of the flesh. Pride,
vanity, self-will, covetousness, independence of
God—these are all lusts of the mind, and they
are just as vile in the sight of God as the lusts
of the flesh. In the first three chapters of the
Epistle to the Romans we have God's picture of
the lusts of the flesh, and in the first three chapters of First Corinthians we have God's picture
of the lusts of the mind. One kind is just as
sinful as the other.

"And were by nature the children of wrath,
even as others." That is, we were born in sin,
we were born of a race that is unclean, unholy,
and obnoxious to the eyes of God, but God had
purposes of grace and of loving-kindness, which
He has carried out through Christ Jesus, for the
salvation of that sinful race.

Do you recognize the picture of your past?
Maybe this is your present instead of your past.
If it is, God grant that it may become your past,
and that you will be through with this kind of
thing forevermore. Life is found alone in Christ.

Now look at the present, as given us in verses
4-6. "But God," how much that expression, *"But
God,"* means. We have God coming in now. We
were dead, helpless, unable to do one thing to re-
trieve our dreadful circumstances, but God came

in. Of old God came in when this world was "without form and void; and darkness was upon the face of the deep . . . and God said, Let there be light: and there was light;" so when we were dead in trespasses and sins, God came in and spoke the word of living power. "But God, who is rich in mercy." In what is He not rich? We saw in the first chapter that He is rich in grace and rich in glory, and here we read that He is rich in mercy. There are infinite resources of mercy for the vilest sinner. There is no one for whom there is no mercy. "God, who is rich in mercy, for His great love wherewith He loved us" —it all came out of the heart of God. There was not a thing about us to commend us to God but, "God so loved the world that He gave His only begotten Son, that whosoever believeth in Him should not perish, but have everlasting life." "In this was manifested the love of God toward us," in that "He sent His only begotten Son into the world, that we might live through Him." "Herein is love, not that we loved God, but that He loved us, and sent His Son to be the propitiation for our sins." Because we were dead, He sent Jesus to give us life; because we were guilty, He sent Jesus to be the propitiation by bearing our sins in His own body on the tree.

"God, who is rich in mercy, for His great love wherewith He loved us, even when we were dead in sins, hath quickened us together with Christ."

The whole human race is dead in trespasses and sins. The Jewish part of the race had the revelation from God, and yet they sought to be justified on the ground of works. But these were dead works, and the Jews were just as truly dead in trespasses and sins as the Gentiles, the great godless world outside. But now God comes in and works in power, and by the living Word He speaks to the dead Jews and to the dead Gentiles, and the Word brings life, and they believe it and are quickened together. They who had been separated before, between whom was a middle wall of partition, are become one in Christ Jesus. That is the meaning of this word, "together." God breaks down the barriers separating Jews and Gentiles and makes them one in Christ through believing, giving us life together *with* Christ. Not merely *in* Christ, but *"with* Christ." Why does He put it that way? There was a time when because of my sins Jesus Christ lay dead in the grave, but, having completed the work that saves, God quickened Him from the dead and brought Him back in triumph from the tomb. Christ's resurrection is the pledge of ours. We believe in Him and are brought forth from the place of the dead and quickened with Him. He is the Saviour, we are the saved, and together we form one blessed company of which He is now the glorified Head.

"By grace ye are saved," and grace precludes all thought of merit. We were not saved because we prayed so earnestly, repented so bitterly, turned over a new leaf, made restitution for past sins, tried to do good, kept the law and obeyed the sermon on the mount, or anything else that we could do, but we were saved by grace, and grace is God's unmerited favor to those who merited the opposite.

In a certain Bible Conference a great number of preachers attended the meetings every day, and some of them were a bit upset because the Conference speaker was telling the people that if they were saved once, they are saved for all eternity. So in trying to press the truth one day, I said, "We are not *being* saved if we hang on to the end, but we have already *been saved*. It is a settled thing." I wish we could understand that.

I am afraid that there are a great many people who imagine that when they come to Christ, it is just the beginning and that they are really on probation; if they keep on and are good enough, they will be saved at last. I cannot understand people who close their prayer with, "Now, O Lord, save us at last." I refuse to say "Amen" to that, for I have already been saved. It is a settled thing, and no one is saved for a time and then becomes unsaved, because in order to become unsaved you would have to become unborn, and how can that be? A saved person has been quickened from the dead, born into the family of God, given a new life, and that life is eternal. If that life could ever be forfeited, it would only be probationary life, dependent upon one's ability to keep it. I have eternal life, and it is not dependent upon my obedience but on the living Christ to see me through to the very end. Do not ever say you are saved if you do not mean that you are saved for eternity. If people ask you if you are saved and you believe you will be saved at last, you will have to say, "Well, not yet; but I hope to be if God and I can only hold out together!" But if you have already trusted the Lord Jesus and believe the Word, say, "Yes, thank God, I am saved for eternity through the precious, atoning blood of the Lord Jesus Christ."

It is one thing to be saved and have eternal life, to be taken out of that state of death, but it is another thing to be presented before God in all the perfection of His blessed Son. It is this of which we read in verse 6, "And hath raised us up together, and made us sit together in heavenly places in Christ Jesus." You notice it is not *with* Christ Jesus. We are quickened with Him —He was quickened from the dead and so we are quickened with Him—but here it says, "He hath raised us up together, and made us sit together in heavenly places in Christ Jesus." Some of these days we shall be caught up and shall be *with* Christ; but that will be when we all get home to glory. While still here, God sees us *in* Christ. We are represented by Him and in Him. As the high priest of old had the names of the Israelites upon his breast and upon his shoulders when he went into that holy place, and they were all seen in their high priest, so we are seen in Christ, and every moment of our lives He is giving us a perfect representation before the throne of God. I am just as truly raised up together and sitting in heavenly places in Christ Jesus when I am lying flat on my back in the hospital as I am when in the meeting. God sees me up there in Christ. Do not drag it down to mere experience. It is a blessed fact that is true of every Christian. It is a great thing to have our experience answer to our standing, and that comes through walking in fellowship with Him.

But what about our future? "That in the ages to come He might show the exceeding riches of His grace in His kindness toward us through Christ Jesus." "The ages to come"—that takes us a long way on, a long way beyond the Millennium. The Millennium is "the age to come," and here we have "the ages to come." That is the Greek expression for eternity. It consists of untold millions of ages running on forevermore. Through all the ages to come God is going to exhibit the exceeding riches of His grace. Some of these days I am going to have a part in a great exhibition, when from the ends of the earth there will be gathered together all the redeemed of the Lord. Then God will demonstrate to all created intelligences how it has been the delight of His heart to show great grace to great sinners. That is our future—a future that does not depend on our faithfulness but on His, who saved us by grace in order that we might show His glories forevermore.

LECTURE IX.

GOD'S WORKMANSHIP

✔ ✔ ✔

"For by grace are ye saved through faith; and that not of yourselves: it is the gift of God: not of works lest any man should boast. For we are His workmanship, created in Christ Jesus unto good works, which God hath before ordained that we should walk in them" (Eph. 2:8-10).

OUR God is very jealous that there should be no slight put upon the Person and work of His blessed Son. God loves poor sinners so much that He sent His Son into the world to be the propitiation for our sins, but He loves His Son so much that He will not permit anyone in heaven who ignores the work that the Lord Jesus Christ accomplished. It is only through His finished work that any of us have title to a place over yonder, and so our salvation is entirely by grace.

As I was meditating on this verse, I thought, "Dear me; what shall I say about it that has not been said a hundred times already?" But it cannot be otherwise, for in trying to present the salvation of God one must dwell on such a passage as this over and over again, for that is the very heart of the matter.

Salvation is entirely by grace, and grace utterly precludes the thought of human merit. Were there any question of merit on our part, it would not be grace. "To him that worketh is the reward not reckoned of grace, but of debt" (Rom. 4:4). If you work, you put the one by whom you are employed into your debt, and he does not get out of your debt until he has paid for your labor. Therefore, if by works of ours, if by any effort of ours, we could earn God's salvation, we would put God in our debt, and He could not get out of it until He had taken us home to heaven as a reward, as payment for what we had done. But no works of ours, no efforts of ours, no labor that we could perform, could ever put away the guilt of one sin; and so we are shut up to grace, to unmerited favor. It is not only unmerited favor, but it is favor against merit, for we have merited the very opposite.

"By grace are ye saved." Notice the apostle does not say, "By grace are ye being saved," or, "By grace will ye be saved eventually," but he is declaring something which is already true of every believer in the Lord Jesus Christ. It is not, "By grace shall ye be saved if ye abide in the present place," but "By grace *are* ye saved," because the work of redemption is already consummated. Therefore, our salvation is looked at by God as something that is finished and complete. If there were any possibility that somehow along the way to heaven I might lose the salvation of God, it could not be said that I am already saved,

but rather that I am being saved. But. thank
God, not only is the work that saves finished, but
the salvation is looked upon as an accomplished
fact. It might be translated. "By grace have ye
been saved."

"Through faith," this is the agent. Faith is
simply the hand that lays hold of the gift that
God presents to me. Believing the gospel, I am
saved. Some people, I think, are in danger of
making a saviour of their faith, for they say,
"Well, if I could only believe firmly enough, if I
could believe in the right way, I think I would
be saved." It is not a question of how you believe; it is a question of whom you believe. Paul
says, "I know whom I have believed, and am per-
suaded that He is able to keep that which I have
committed unto Him against that day" (2 Tim.
1:12). Do not make a saviour of your faith.
The Saviour is Christ, and faith lays hold of Him.
Then lest there should be any idea in the mind of
the redeemed one that in some sense at any rate
he deserves credit for coming to Christ and believing this message, the apostle immediately
adds, "And that not of yourselves: it is the gift
of God."

Take the message as a whole again, "By grace
are ye saved through faith; and that not of yourselves: it is the gift of God." Theologians have
questioned as to whether "not of yourselves"
means the salvation or the faith. We may apply

it to the whole subject in question, "By grace are ye saved, and that not of yourselves." The grace, the salvation, are not of yourselves. "By grace are ye saved through faith, and that not of yourselves." The faith is not of yourselves; it is all the gift of God. But somebody says, "If faith is the gift of God and God is not pleased to give me that gift, how can I believe?" Scripture says, "Faith cometh by hearing, and hearing by the Word of God." God gives the gift of faith to all who give heed to the message of the gospel. After the Spirit of God brings that message home to the heart, it is thoroughly possible for men to resist the Holy Ghost. It is possible on the other hand to give heed to the ministry of the Spirit, and thus be led on to personal faith in the Lord Jesus Christ. Faith is a gift, and apart from it you can never be saved, but in order that we may have faith, "God so loved the world, that He gave His only begotten Son, that whosoever believeth in Him should not perish, but have everlasting life." Refuse the Word, and there will never be faith; give heed to the Word, and faith cometh by hearing. And so of it all it may be said, "Not of works, lest any man should boast."

Old John Nelson, one of Wesley's preachers, was a poor, godless, blaspheming blacksmith until God saved him, and after that he became one of the early Methodist preachers, and proclaimed in

power the gospel of the grace of God and won
many to a saving knowledge of the Lord Jesus
Christ. One day he was talking to a very self-
righteous man who said, "I don't need your
Saviour; my life is all I need. I can present my
own life to God, and I am satisfied He won't be
hard on me. If anybody gets into heaven I shall,
because of the good I have done, because of the
way I have lived." "Look here," said John Nelson; "if you got into heaven, you would bring discord there. All in heaven will be saved sinners,
and we are going to sing, 'Glory to the Lamb that
was slain and hath washed us from our sins in
His own blood.' You couldn't sing that, and so
you would bring discord. You would be singing,
'Glory to me because by my own good life and
consistent living, my charity and good behavior,
I fitted myself for heaven.' If the angels caught
you doing that, they would take you by the nape
of your neck and throw you over the wall." That
is a rather crude way of putting it, but he knew
the truth of salvation by grace. David says, "My
soul shall make her boast in the Lord." I have
no goodness of my own, no faithfulness, no merit,
but I shall boast in Him.

In the tenth verse we read, "For we are His
workmanship, created in Christ Jesus unto good
works, which God hath before ordained that we
should walk in them." The word translated
"workmanship" is used only twice in the New

Testament, here in Ephesians and in the first
chapter of Romans where Paul is speaking of the
testimony of creation. He says in verse 20, "For
the invisible things of Him from the creation of
the world are clearly seen, being understood by
the things that are made, even His eternal power
and Godhead; so that they are without excuse."
In the original, one Greek word is translated here,
"the things that are made." That word is *poiema*.
From it we get our English word "poem." Creation is God's poem, witnessing to His eternal
power and glory. The very stars in the heaven
are,

> "Forever singing as they shine,
> The hand that made us is divine."

That word is used again only in this second chapter of the Epistle to the Ephesians, and here it is
translated "workmanship," which means something that someone has made. So we read that,
"We are His workmanship (we are His poem),
created in Christ Jesus unto good works."

What a wonderful piece of literature a poem is!
How different from any prose! It takes a man
or woman of a peculiar cast of mind to produce
a worthwhile poem. There is something artistic
about it, and all the hard work in the world could
not enable you to produce one unless you have the
poetic instinct. It is a very artistic thing to play
an organ, and I might sit down and work away on

it from now until I became decrepit and aged, but I would never get music out of it because I have no music in me. You have to be a musician in order to bring the music out of an organ, and you have to be a poet in order to write poems. If God were other than He is, He never could have brought this universe into existence nor saved one poor sinner. Creation is God's first poem, but redemption is His second poem, and you and I who are saved constitute the syllables in God's great poem of redemption. Every one is set in the right place by God Himself, "We are His workmanship," and therefore He is given all the credit, for He has done it all through His Son.

We are created in Christ Jesus, quickened unto newness of life with Him and represented before God in Him—"Created in Christ Jesus unto good works." Notice the order. He has already told us that we are not saved by good works, but now says that we must not ignore good works, for one of the purposes for which He has saved us is in order that we might do good works. In the general epistles there are two great sayings: "This is a faithful saying, and worthy of all acceptation, that Christ Jesus came into the world to save sinners" (1 Tim. 1:15). But in Titus 3:8 we read, "This is a faithful saying, and these things I will that thou affirm constantly, that they which have believed in God might be careful to maintain good works. These things are good and profitable unto

men." You see the place good works have, they are
not to be ignored, but they are not meritorious.
We are not saved by them, but we are created in
Christ Jesus *unto* good works.   In other words,
springing from the fact that we have been saved,
because we are God's workmanship, God's great
redemptive poem, our lives should now be musical, should be rhythmical and lyrical, and every
one of us should fit into the place where He has
set us in this great epic of redemption.

"We are His workmanship, created in Christ
Jesus unto good works, which God hath before
ordained that we should walk in them."   Do you
believe in foreordination?   If you are a Christian,
you are foreordained to behave yourself, to do
good works, to live a life well pleasing unto God.
That is what He has marked out for you.   The
Christian's pathway is a life lived in subjection to
Him.

MADE NIGH BY THE BLOOD
OF CHRIST

✓ ✓ ✓

"Wherefore remember, that ye being in time past Gentiles in the flesh, who are called Uncircumcision by that which is called the Circumcision in the flesh made by hands; that at that time ye were without Christ, being aliens from the commonwealth of Israel, and strangers from the covenants of promise, having no hope, and without God in the world: but now in Christ Jesus ye who sometimes were far off are made nigh by the blood of Christ. For He is our peace, who hath made both one, and hath broken down the middle wall of partition between us; having abolished in His flesh the enmity, even the law of commandments contained in ordinances; for to make in Himself of twain one new man, so making peace; and that He might reconcile both unto God in one body by the cross, having slain the enmity thereby: and came and preached peace to you which were afar off, and to them that were nigh. For through Him we both have access by one Spirit unto the Father" (Eph. 2: 11-18).

✓ ✓ ✓

WE have already taken up the question of the past, present and future of the individual believer. In this passage, the apostle addresses converted Gentiles collectively and speaks of converted Jews collectively. He says in verse 11, "Wherefore remember, that ye being in time past Gentiles in the flesh, who are called

Uncircumcision by that which is called the Circumcision in the flesh made by hands: that at that time ye were without Christ, being aliens from the commonwealth of Israel, and strangers from the covenants of promise, having no hope, and without God in the world."

Of old God had called one man, Abraham, out from the world and made him the depositary of certain promises. Afterwards He gave to his seed the covenant of works, the Mosaic covenant at Mt.Sinai, and by that God separated the people of Israel from all the other people of the world. Those outside of Israel were called Gentiles. It is a remarkable thing that in the Old Testament God is never said to have made a covenant with the Gentiles as such. After the days of Noah, His covenants were all made with Israel, and His promises were all made to Israel. He made many wonderful promises *about* the Gentiles, but He made none to them, and therefore, when Christ came into the world and the gospel first began to be preached, it could be said that those who were Gentiles in the flesh, like ourselves, "were without Christ, being aliens from the commonwealth of Israel, and strangers from the covenants of promise, having no hope, and without God in the world."

Israel had a very definite hope. God had promised certain things to them. But the Gentiles had no such hope, they were outside of all this, and therefore without God in the world. It was not merely that they worshiped idols, that they bowed down to gods of wood and stone, but the point was they did not know the true God at all. They were godless, "atheists," in the world. But now, through the coming of our Lord Jesus Christ and through His death on Calvary's cross, wondrous blessing flows forth to the nations of the Gentiles, blessings of which they had never dared to dream in the past.

"Now in Christ Jesus ye who sometimes were far off are made nigh by the blood of Christ." You see the Jew occupied a place of nearness to God through covenant relationship, while the Gentile was far off, being a stranger to it all. But the Jew through his failure to keep his part of the covenant of works, had himself become personally alienated from God, so that, after all, in His sight, as we read in the Epistle to the Romans, "There is no difference, for all have sinned, and come short of the glory of God." Therefore, the same grace that flowed out to Israel is the grace that overflows to the Gentiles. The Jews never obtained salvation on the ground of merit, or because they were God's peculiar people marked off from the nations of the world by the covenant of circumcision, nor because of the sacrifices which they offered throughout the legal dispensation. Those of them who were saved owed everything to the matchless grace of God which gave the

Lord Jesus Christ, their promised Messiah, to die for their sins upon that cross of shame. And that same mighty Sacrifice which was offered upon the tree avails for all men everywhere who put their trust in Him. And so, although no covenant has been made with the Gentiles, although the new covenant of which we read in Jeremiah and in Hebrews is never said to have been made with the Church, but is to be made with Israel and Judah in the last days, yet every believing Gentile comes under all the spiritual blessings of the new covenant the moment he trusts in Christ, because it is all pure grace.

The shedding of the blood of our Lord Jesus Christ was the greatest crime ever perpetrated on the face of this earth. It involved the awful sin of deicide. When a man murders another, he is held responsible for taking the life of his fellow-man, but when a man stretches forth his hand against God incarnate, what can be said about his guilt! Yet that is the awful crime in which Jews and Gentiles participated. When the Lord Jesus Christ was nailed to Calvary's tree and His blood poured forth, it was the manifestation of the world's greatest sin, but it also became the greatest possible manifestation of the infinite love and grace of God. That which declares the enormity of man's sin and the corruption of his heart is that which manifests the love of God to the greatest extent. All this was foreseen.

Peter could say, "Him, being delivered by the determinate counsel and foreknowledge of God, ye have taken, and by wicked hands have crucified and slain" (Acts 2:23). Yet this same Jesus is now made Lord and Christ, and through Him all who believe, as the Apostle Paul says, "are justified from all things." We sometimes sing:

> "The very spear that pierced His side
> Drew forth the blood to save."

That Roman spear-point driven into the very heart of the Son of God tells out the wickedness of the heart of man, but that cleansing blood rushing forth to wash away our sins tells how God has loved us, how wonderfully the grace of God has abounded over all our sins. We who sometimes were far off, we poor, wretched Gentiles, alienated from God by wicked works, and enemies in our minds, have now by putting our trust in Him been brought into a place of nearness that the law could never give even to Jews, and the Jew who believes in Him has been brought into this same blessed place. Together we have been "made nigh by the blood of Christ."

The blood of beasts that was shed of old could never settle the sin question because there was not sufficient intrinsic value in the victim, but in the case of our Lord Jesus Christ we see the Holy, the Just, the Sovereign of the skies, stooping to man's estate. He had to be who He is in

order to do what He did, and because He is the
infinite God become Man His blood has atoning
value that no other blood could have. Thus we
are made "nigh by the blood of Christ." We may
well sing:

> "So near, so very near, to God,
>   Nearer I could not be;
> For in the person of His Son,
>   I am as near as He.
>
> "So dear, so very dear, to God,
>   Dearer I could not be;
> The love wherewith He loves the Son,
>   Such is His love to me."

Dear Christian, does your heart enter into it?
Do you realize that the very moment you came, a
feeble trembling sinner, and reached out the hand
of faith, laid hold of the testimony of God concerning His blessed Son, that moment by the
precious blood of Christ you were brought into
such an intimate relationship to God that you
could not be drawn any closer? Of course, when
it comes to communion that is another thing, for
in that sense there are times when we are nearer
to Him than at others. But we have been "made
nigh by the blood of Christ." Not made nigh by
the sincerity of our repentance, by the strength
of our faith, by the depth of our devotion, by the
gladness of our spiritual experience, but made
nigh by the blood. We owe everything for eter-

nity to the precious atoning blood of our blessed
Lord, and He who shed that blood, He who died
for our sins upon the cross, is Himself our peace.

We read, "Being justified by faith, we have
peace with God." That is not merely an experience of calmness in the soul, but it is the blessed
realization that the sin question has been fully
settled, that that which separated between our
souls and God has been done away, done away in
the cross, and so Christ Himself is our peace. You
see I am not called upon to be occupied with my
feelings, but with Christ. I may be very happy
today, and then circumstances may arise tomorrow which cause the clouds to overshadow my
soul and hide the sunshine of God's face, and I
may be in darkness, doubt, difficulty, and perplexity, but my peace remains unchanged.

> "Peace with God is Christ in glory,
>   God is just and God is love;
> Jesus died to tell the story,
>   Foes to bring to God above."

And so when I get disgusted with myself and
my own poor experience, I can look away from
self and look up by faith to Him, the blessed
Christ of God seated there on the right hand of
the Majesty in heaven, and say, "Yonder is my
peace, my heart rests in Him. God rests in Him,
and I rest in Him." Has your soul entered into
it? I hope we make these things practical, so

that they do not become mere doctrinal statements to us but realities that sink into the depths
of our beings.

"For He is our peace, who hath made both
one." What does He mean by, "Hath made both
one?" Does He mean that He hath made Christ
and us one? That is blessedly true, but that is
not what is spoken of here. He was speaking
a little farther back of two opposite companies,
the circumcision and the uncircumcision, the Jew
and the Gentile, the covenant people and those
who are strangers to the covenants of promise.
But when Christ died, He died for both, and we
who believe from both of these companies are
now reconciled to God, and therefore we read,
"He hath made both one." And so my Jewish
brother and I, his Gentile brother, are one in
Christ.

"And hath broken down the middle wall of partition between us." I think the apostle is referring, as an illustration, at any rate, to the wall in
the temple of old, separating the court of the
Gentiles from the court of the Israelites. On this
wall there was an inscription which was dug up
just a few years ago, and it read, "Let no Gentile,
let no man of the nations, go beyond this wall on
pain of death." But the apostle says, "He hath
broken down the middle wall of partition between
us."

"Having abolished in His flesh the enmity, even

the law of commandments contained in ordinances; for to make in Himself of twain one new man, so making peace." What does he mean by that new man? It is the Body consisting of redeemed Jews and Gentiles here on earth and our glorious Head, our Lord Jesus Christ, in heaven. Redeemed sinners united by the Holy Spirit to Christ in heaven from now on form one new man, and so in a double sense peace has been made between the individual soul and God, and between Jew and Gentile, once separated by this middle wall of partition. In order that peace might be made between the individual soul and God, the law of commandments contained in ordinances had to be abolished.

That law pronounced a curse and condemnation on all who violated it. It was the Jews' pride and boasting that they were custodians of the law of God, and so they were, and yet they did not realize that it but put them all under the curse. They thought they were a blessed people and a privileged people to have the law of God, but alas, alas, they had broken the law, and God said, "Cursed is every one that continueth not in all things that are written in the book of the law to do them" (Gal. 3:10). But the blessed Lord Jesus went to the cross and was made a curse for us—"As it is written, Cursed is every one that hangeth on a tree" (Gal. 3:13). And so by enduring the cross, by bearing the judgment, He has "abolished in His flesh the law of commandments contained in ordinances." And now both Jews and Gentiles come to God on the same basis, as sinners, but as sinners for whom Christ died. Out of these two companies, when redeemed, you have the new man of which Christ is the Head.

Then in verse 16 he uses the other term, "In one Body," and says, "That He might reconcile both unto God in one body by the cross, having slain the enmity thereby." He has slain the enmity by taking our place upon the cross and bearing the judgment for us. We read that He has made in Himself of Jew and Gentile one new man. That takes in, as we have said, the Body on earth and the Head in Heaven. Now we read, "That He might reconcile both unto God in one Body." Why not say, "That He might reconcile both unto God in one new man"? It is because Christ does not have to be reconciled to God, but the Body must be reconciled to Him, for we who form the Body were all poor sinners, we were once on our way to everlasting ruin, but we have been reconciled unto God in one Body. How are we reconciled to God? You remember, our blessed Lord came into the world to manifest the love of God to sinners, and we read, "God was in Christ reconciling the world unto Himself." But what was the result? Did men receive Him gladly? Did they own Him as Saviour and Lord? Instead of that they nailed Him to the cross of shame. But

love that was stronger than death, love that the
many waters of judgment could not quench, led
Him to go down into the darkness of the tomb
for us, and now through faith in the risen Christ
who died for our sins, the enmity has been ban-
ished and we have been reconciled to God. And
so in resurrection power, having settled the sin
question, having completed the work that makes
atonement, the blessed Lord returned to this very
world that rejected Him. He appeared here for
forty days in His resurrection body, and gave the
message of the gospel to His disciples to carry
into the world. He "came and preached peace."
He sent forth the good news of peace to you which
were afar off, poor sinners of the Gentiles dying
in ignorance and darkness, and to you which were
nigh, Jews to whom His Word had come, who
had the oracles of God, who had light that the
Gentiles knew nothing of, but who joined with the
Gentiles in crucifying the Lord of glory. In the
love of His heart the message goes to you as well
as to the world outside. He "came and preached
peace to you which were afar off, and to them
that were nigh."

In the next verse we have a wonderful statement: "For through Him—" Through whom?
The resurrected Christ who ever lives at God's
right hand to make intercession for us. "For
through Him we both" (that is, we Jews and we
Gentiles who were once far off) now "have ac-

cess by one Spirit unto the Father." Of old there was no immediate access to God. That unrent vail told of a God hidden in the dark. God was not able to come out to man because of the fact that the sin question was not settled, and man could not go in to God for there was no way for his sins to be cleansed. But now the death of Christ has rent the separating vail.

"The vail is rent! Our souls draw near
Unto a throne of grace;
The merits of the Lord appear,
They fill the holy place.

"His precious blood has spoken there,
Before and on the throne:
And His own wounds in heaven declare,
The atoning work is done.

" 'Tis finished! Here our souls have rest,
His work can never fail:
By Him, our Sacrifice and Priest,
We pass within the vail.

"Within the holiest of all,
Cleansed by His precious blood,
Before the throne we prostrate fall,
And worship Thee, O God!"

Through Him we both have access, immediate access, by one Spirit, the Holy Spirit, who was given by God at Pentecost, baptizing believing Jews and Gentiles into one Body, and has made us both members of this one new man. We both have access by one Spirit unto the Father. What a wonderful thing it is to be a Christian! What a wonderful thing it is not only to have your sins forgiven but to have been brought into the family of God, and to have been made a fellow-member with other believers of the Body of Christ. Not only that, but to be accepted of God and to be as near to the heart of God as His own beloved Son. Not only that, but to have immediate access at any moment into His own blessed presence within the holiest in the power of the Holy Spirit. And all this rests on the infinite value of the blood of the Lord Jesus Christ. "Made nigh by the blood of Christ."

BUILT TOGETHER FOR A HABITATION OF GOD

✦ ✦ ✦

"Now therefore ye are no more strangers and foreigners, but fellow-citizens with the saints, and of the household of God; and are built upon the foundation of the apostles and prophets, Jesus Christ Himself being the chief corner stone; in whom all the building fitly framed together groweth unto an holy temple in the Lord: in whom ye also are builded together for an habitation of God through the Spirit" (Eph. 2:19-22).

✦ ✦ ✦

IN this second chapter we have had brought before us in a very vivid way our relationship to the Father as those who have been quickened together with Christ. We have been regenerated, we have been made members of the family of God, the same divine life having been communicated to every one of us, and thus we are brought into this living relationship with the Father. And then we have seen our new relationship to Christ. We are now made members of His Body. The Body of Christ is looked at in Scripture in two very distinct aspects. First, as comprising all believers from Pentecost to the coming again of our Lord Jesus Christ to call us all to meet Him in the air. In other words, all

saints of this dispensation constitute the Body of
Christ. But then it is looked at in another way.
In Corinthians it is the aggregate of believers
upon the earth at a given time. All Christians
today constitute the Body of Christ as now manifest in the world, and all Christians throughout
the entire dispensation constitute the Body of
Christ as it will be for all eternity. We saw that
in the Body of Christ all distinctions between
Jews and Gentiles who believe in the Lord Jesus
Christ are done away, the middle wall of partition is broken down, and we are one in Him.

Now we go on to consider our relationship to
the Holy Spirit, and find that we have been constituted a habitation in which God by the Holy
Spirit dwells during the time of our sojourn on
the earth, and in which He will dwell throughout
all the ages to come. Two different figures are
used, one the Tabernacle, as set forth in the book
of Exodus, and the other the glorious Temple, as
depicted for us in the books of Kings and Chron-
icles. The Tabernacle represents the temporary
condition, the Temple the eternal condition which
will abide forever, and so we read in verse 19,
"Now therefore ye are no more strangers and
foreigners, but fellow-citizens with the saints, and
of the household of God."

We have noticed in our earlier study that
throughout this letter the apostle says "ye" when
he is addressing Gentiles and "we" when he

speaks of Jews. He was a Jewish believer, and
speaks of "we who first hoped in Christ," and
then speaks of "ye who also trusted, after that
ye heard the word of truth, the gospel of your
salvation." So now he says, "Ye are no more
strangers and foreigners, but fellow-citizens with
the saints, and of the household of God." We
have seen that the Gentiles were "strangers from
the covenants of promise." They were outside,
they did not belong to that special elect nation of
Israel, but alas, many in Israel failed to enter
into their holy privilege, and so we are told elsewhere that they are not all Israel who are of
Israel, but God called out a remnant from Israel,
and that remnant by accepting the Lord Jesus
Christ as their Saviour were baptized into Jesus
Christ and were made living stones in the house
of God. And now Gentiles who believe, though
having no part nor lot in this matter, are brought
in, too, and are no longer "strangers and foreigners, but fellow-citizens with the saints."

What do we mean by "saints"? Simply that
we are now linked with Israel after the flesh? Not
at all. They forfeited all rights from an earthly
standpoint. It is those in Israel who believe in
the Lord Jesus Christ who are here called saints,
and so when he says we are "fellow-citizens with
the saints," he means that the Gentiles who believe in the Lord Jesus Christ are as truly united
to Christ now by the Spirit as our Jewish breth-

ren who believe in the same blessed Saviour. A "saint" is a holy one, but holiness is not a question primarily of experience. A "holy one" is one set apart to God. People often think of saints as those who have already attained to perfect holiness, but that is not the divine thought at all. Every one who puts his trust in the blessed Lord has been set apart to God in Christ, and thus is constituted a saint. But now having been made a saint, one is called upon to live in a saintly way. We do not become saints by holy living, but because God has constituted us saints we are called to holy living.

So we read that we have been made "fellow-citizens with the saints." What citizenship is that? It is a heavenly citizenship. We read in Philippians, "Our citizenship is in heaven." Philippi was what the Romans called a colony, but they used that term in a different sense from what we use it today. A Roman colony was a city that had been characterized by some special devotedness to the Roman imperial government, and in order to reward the citizens of that place for their loyalty and faithfulness the title "Colonia" was conferred upon that city. That meant that from that time on every free-born person living in that place was constituted a Roman citizen, and had just exactly the same rights and privileges as though he were free born in Rome.

It was some years before Paul wrote that letter

to the Philippians that the Romans were in conflict with the people to the north and to the east of Macedonia, and when the Roman legions reached Philippi they found the citizens of that place had already raised a great army to assist, and had provided vast resources to meet the army. So delighted was the Roman general with their generosity and loyalty that he sent back to Rome a splendid report. The Senate then met and conferred upon them the title "Colonia," which means that every Philippian could then say, "I am a Roman citizen." However, Philippi was in Macedonia, and of course the people had certain duties to that government, but Philippi was governed directly from Rome, and had a representative of the Roman government there. See how the apostle applies it here. We are in this world sinners saved by grace and linked to our blessed Lord Jesus Christ, though He is rejected by this world. And now God so appreciates devotion to His blessed Son in this the day of His rejection, that He says, "I am going to confer upon every one who trusts Him, upon every one who owns His Lordship during this time when the world is spurning Him, the title of 'Colonia.' They are heavenly citizens; they belong to heaven." Though in the world, we are "fellow-citizens with the saints." We have our duties, our responsibilities to the world in which we live, but our prime duty, our prime responsibility, is to heaven with which we have to do because we are citizens of that blessed country and belong to the household of God.

Now he uses the figure of a building, and says, "And are built upon the foundation of the apostles and prophets, Jesus Christ Himself being the chief corner stone." You remember this same figure is used in other places in the New Testament. In the third chapter of First Corinthians we read of the building that God is erecting in the wonderful gospel days. You have it again in the sixth chapter of Second Corinthians where we read of the temple of God, and also in the second chapter of the first epistle of Peter, where believers are likened to living stones built upon *the* Living Stone, our Lord Jesus Christ.

In the Old Testament when Solomon's temple was erected on Mount Moriah, in order that there might be a level platform upon which the great superstructure should stand, vast stones were brought and mortared into the solid rock, and then stones were fitted into that temple. At the end of seven years it was the most wonderful sanctuary that the world had ever known up to that time. But there was a peculiarity about the construction. It went up without the sound of a hammer, because the stones were quarried out below; they were also cut, shaped and polished down there, and then placed upon that platform and cemented together without the use of a work-

man's hammer. So today no one can hear a
sound as a living stone is fitted into the temple
of God, but God by the Holy Ghost is quarrying
out these living stones from the depths of sin, and
He is lifting them up by His mighty power and
building them upon Christ, the great foundation.

> "View the vast building, see it rise!
> The work how great, the plan how wise!
> Nor can that faith be overthrown
> That rests upon the Living Stone."

Some day this temple will be completed, but
it is now in course of construction. Every believer is a living stone. In Africa, India, China,
and the islands of the sea, God is finding these
living stones and they are being built into this
glorious structure. It will remain for eternity the
glorious sanctuary in which God will display the
riches of His grace to all created intelligences.
What a wonderful thing to be a living stone in
that temple! You see no man can make himself
a living stone, only the Spirit of God can do that,
and therefore it is only those who have believed
in the Lord Jesus Christ who are placed in this
wonderful building.

"And are built upon the foundation of the
apostles and prophets, Jesus Christ Himself being
the chief corner stone." Does he mean that the
apostles and prophets are the foundation? Not
at all. He means that they are built upon the

foundation that they laid. What foundation did they lay? Paul says, "Other foundation can no man lay than that is laid, which is Jesus Christ" (1 Cor. 3:11). So the apostles and the prophets proclaimed the truth concerning the Lord Jesus Christ, and upon that foundation this glorious temple is being builded. You say, "But what prophets are these? We have no difficulty about the apostles for we know they are the apostles of the new dispensation. Do the prophets include the Old Testament prophets?" We answer, They preached Christ. Who preached a more glorious gospel than Isaiah? Listen to His wonderful words, "He was wounded for our transgressions, He was bruised for our iniquities: the chastisement of our peace was upon Him; and with His stripes we are healed." Listen to Jeremiah, "This is His name whereby He shall be called, The Lord our Righteousness" (Jer. 23:6). Listen to Zechariah, "Awake, O sword, against My Shepherd, and against the Man that is My Fellow, saith the Lord of hosts: smite the Shepherd, and the sheep shall be scattered: and I will turn Mine hand upon the little ones" (Zech. 13:7). And so we might go on. In this sense the prophets of the Old Testament joined with the apostles of the New Testament in setting forth the truth of a crucified and risen Saviour, but if he had in mind these Old Testament prophets, we might expect him to say "prophets and apostles," for these Old Testament prophets came long before the apostles did. But, you see, he reverses it and says, "And are built upon the foundation of the apostles and prophets." Would it not be rather this that just as there were apostles of the New Testament dispensation so there were also the prophets? We read, for instance, of certain prophets and teachers at Antioch. Some of the writers of the New Testament, as Mark and Luke, were not apostles but were prophets, and so I take it that we are to limit this to the New Testament workmen, those who were raised up of God at the beginning to lay the foundation, to preach Christ, to proclaim the gospel. It is upon this glorious proclamation that the temple of God has been building through the centuries.

"Built upon the foundation of the apostles and prophets, Jesus Christ Himself being the chief corner stone." "There is none other name under heaven given among men, whereby we must be saved" (Acts 4:12). Christ is the One Mediator between God and man. Only those who put their trust in Him are built into this holy temple. Only those who have been saved through His death, His shed blood, and His glorious resurrection are members of His Body. Only those who have rested their souls for eternity upon the work that He accomplished upon Calvary have been quickened together with Him and are thus brought into the family of God. These are our brethren. Others

are our fellow-men, in whom we are deeply interested, over whom we yearn with the compassion of Christ. But we dare not take that sacred
term of "brethren" and apply it those who reject
our Lord Jesus Christ, who trample His blood
under their feet, for it is upon His work alone
we rest. We remember He said to Peter, "Whom
say ye that I am?" and Peter answered, "Thou art
the Christ, the Son of the living God." And Jesus
said, "Blessed art thou, Simon Bar-jona: for flesh
and blood hath not revealed it unto thee but My
Father which is in heaven. And I say unto thee,
that thou art Peter, and upon this rock I will
build My Church." What rock? That Christ is
the Son of the living God. "On this rock I will
build My Church." This is the one foundation.
It was laid in death when Jesus died upon the
tree and now in resurrection the Spirit is building
this glorious temple upon Christ.

But now, as we said, the temple is not yet finished. As long as there are still poor sinners to
be brought in, the temple is not complete. If you
should ask for my opinion as to how near we are
to the finished temple, I would say that I think
there are a very few more stones to be put in,
just one here and there in the roof, and then it
will be complete. It might be that the last living
stone to be placed in the building will be placed
there today, and then the work will be done.

"In whom all the building, fitly framed to-

gether," that is, every one is fitted by the Holy
Spirit into his or her exact place as a living stone.
"In whom all the building fitly framed together
groweth—that is progress, not completion, it is
not that it has grown up but—"groweth unto an
holy temple in the Lord." And when it is all completed, what a dwelling-place for God and the
Lamb it will be. What a wonderful sanctuary
through all the ages to come. When you think of
being a living stone in that glorious building,
does it not bring to your soul a sense of the importance of holy living, of devotedness to Christ,
of so behaving yourself that He will delight in
dwelling in you? Whereas in 1 Corinthians 3
and 2 Corinthians 6 the temple of God is the entire Church, in 1 Corinthians 6 the temple of the
Holy Spirit is the individual. In 1 Corinthians
3:16 we read, "Know ye not that ye are the temple of God, and that the Spirit of God dwelleth
in you?" And then speaking of the enemies outside, he says, "If any man defile the temple of
God, him shall God destroy; for the temple of
God is holy, which temple ye are." In 2 Corinthians 6:16 we read, "What agreement hath the
temple of God with idols? for ye are the temple
of the living God; as God hath said, I will dwell
in them, and walk in them; and I will be their
God, and they shall be My people." And it is because the Church collectively comprises the temple of God that the command comes, "Wherefore

come out from among them, and be ye separate,
saith the Lord, and touch not the unclean thing;
and I will receive you." But now look back at 1
Corinthians 6:19. You will find that he changes
the figure to the individual. "What? Know ye
not that your body is the temple of the Holy
Ghost which is in you, which ye have of God, and
ye are not your own?" Here we find the word is,
"your body," not "your bodies." The individual
is the temple of the Holy Ghost which is in him.
Addressing the whole company he says that collectively they form the temple of God but each individual believer's body is the temple of the Holy
Ghost. What godliness should characterize us,
what piety, what separation from the world, what
faithfulness to Christ should mark us!

Coming back to verses 20, 21 of Ephesians 2,
the temple is spoken of, but in verse 22 we have,
I believe, the thought of the tabernacle. He has
been speaking of the whole company of believers,
and now comes back to address any group of believers at a given time, like this church at
Ephesus. "In whom ye also are builded together
for an habitation of God through the Spirit."
That is a finished product right here on the earth,
like the tabernacle which could be placed at a
given place today, taken down tomorrow, and
moved elsewhere. It was made of a number of
boards which had been fitted together, covered
with gold, and united by bands. Then on each

board there were two tenons which went down into sockets of silver. Beautiful curtains covered the united framework. Once those boards had been trees out in the desert, as you and I were poor sinners having no hope in the world, cut down by the work of the Spirit of God, planed and fitted together by the Spirit and now made the abiding place of God. They were covered with gold—made the righteousness of God in Christ. The curtains speak of all His perfections sheltering His own. This is the picture that is used here. You as a company of Christians are builded together for an habitation of God through the Spirit.

Do we realize this as much as we should? Any assembly or church of the living God (and I use this in the strictest New Testament sense, a company of called-out believers) is the habitation of God through the Spirit. That is why the Church should be kept holy, that is why unsaved people should have no part in its fellowship, because they are not members of the true Church. That is why Christians who are members of that Church should be careful to eschew all worldliness and everything that would dishonor the Lord Jesus Christ. May God give us to so live that we shall glorify His name in this scene.

LECTURE XII.

THE REVELATION OF THE MYSTERY

✓ ✓ ✓

"For this cause I Paul, the prisoner of Jesus Christ for you Gentiles, if ye have heard of the dispensation of the grace of God which is given me to you-ward: how that by revelation He made known unto me the mystery; (as I wrote afore in few words, whereby, when ye read, ye may understand my knowledge in the mystery of Christ) which in other ages was not made known unto the sons of men, as it is now revealed unto His holy apostles and prophets by the Spirit; that the Gentiles should be fellow-heirs, and of the same Body, and partakers of His promise in Christ by the gospel: whereof I was made a minister, according to the gift of the grace of God given unto me by the effectual working of His power. Unto me, who am less than the least of all saints, is this grace given, that I should preach among the Gentiles the unsearchable riches of Christ; and to make all men see what is the fellowship of the mystery, which from the beginning of the world hath been hid in God, who created all things by Jesus Christ: to the intent that now unto the principalities and powers in heavenly places might be known by the Church the manifold wisdom of God, according to the eternal purpose which He purposed in Christ Jesus our Lord: in whom we have boldness and access with confidence by the faith of Him. Wherefore I desire that ye faint not at my tribulations for you, which is your glory" (Eph. 3: 1-13).

✓ ✓ ✓

THE apostle comes now to the unfolding of that great secret which had been in the heart of God from eternity, but in this glorious dispensation of grace has at last been fully revealed. It is my thought we should see that in a very special sense Paul was the chosen one to make known this mystery in all its fulness. On the other hand we need to guard against the idea that no others participated in this knowledge, for in verse 5 of the portion we have just read we note that he declares, "It is now revealed unto His holy apostles and prophets by the Spirit." Others, therefore, shared with him in this blessed knowledge, but preeminently he was the apostle of the mystery.

No one else speaks of the Body of Christ, among all the New Testament writers. To Paul this revelation came first that he might communicate it to others. But the truth that Jew and Gentile were to be blessed alike on the ground of pure grace was made known to the twelve. Our Lord sets forth this truth in John 10: 4, 16. "His own sheep" from the Jewish fold, and "other sheep" of the Gentiles were to form "one flock" under the fostering care of "one Shepherd." Peter's vision of the sheet let down from heaven set forth the same glorious mystery. But the revelation of the one Body was the special truth committed to Paul and made known in germ at the very time of his conversion, as the words, "Why persecutest thou Me?" imply. To touch a saint on earth was to touch the Head in heaven. Thus was he taught the unity of the Body and its union with the glorified Head.

We might say it was because of this very truth
that he was in prison at the time he wrote the
Ephesian letter. This I think is involved in the
expression "I, Paul, the prisoner of Jesus Christ
for you Gentiles." You will remember that in
his defence on the temple stairs at Jerusalem, it
was when he announced that he had been commanded by the Lord to go unto the Gentiles that
the ire of his Jewish hearers was stirred to the
depths, and they cried, "Away with such a fellow
from the earth; it is not fit for him to live." We,
therefore, who are Gentiles by nature, have special reason to be grateful to Paul for his faithfulness in proclaiming the purpose of God concerning our part in the divine program. Because of
this he suffered obliquy and shame, and spent
many weary months in prison rather than sur-
render in the least degree the truth of God committed to him.

Here, as in Colossians, he indicates that his
was a double ministry. First, he speaks (ver. 2)
of the dispensation of the grace of God which was
given him. A dispensation, as we have seen, is a
stewardship. Paul, like every true New Testament
preacher, was a steward of the grace of God.
Notice how the Apostle Peter also speaks in his
first epistle, 4:10, "As every man has received
the gift, even so minister the same one to another
as good stewards of the manifold grace of God."
Grace, we have already observed, is God's un-

merited favor to those who have deserved the very opposite. It is this that is proclaimed in the gospel. And this, of course, is the first part of the mystery. The apostle goes on to show that he was not only a minister of the gospel, but in a special sense a minister of this now revealed secret.

He says that by revelation the mystery was made known to him, and he calls it the "mystery of Christ." It is God's wonderful secret concerning the glory of His blessed Son. How good it is to know that Christ's glory and our salvation are eternally linked and can never be separated. Speaking of the mystery he says, "As I wrote afore in few words." This, I take it, refers to what he had already said in chapter 1: 9-13. He will now elaborate that more fully. He had also written before to others concerning this mystery, as, for instance, to the Romans in chapter 16: 25, 26; to the Corinthians, see the first epistle, chapter 2: 7; and in others of his letters we have similar references. I mention this because of the unwarranted position taken by some that the mystery was never revealed until Paul's imprisonment. On the contrary, he had been proclaiming it from the very beginning, both by voice and pen.

Now what is this mystery which in other ages was hidden from the sons of men? We are told in verse 6: "That the Gentiles should be fellow-heirs and of the same Body, and partakers of His promise in Christ by the gospel." In what does this differ from the Old Testament declaration that God would bless the Gentiles through Israel? The great difference, I take it, is this: According to the Old Testament prophets the day is coming when Israel will be restored to covenant relationship with God and will be brought into a place of special blessing here on the earth, and the Gentile nations living at that time will be blessed with and in subjection to them. But the great truth for our age is, that God is now calling out a people for the heavens to be the Body and Bride of His Son throughout the ages to come, and through whom He will administer the affairs of a redeemed universe. This Body is composed of those who were once by nature Jews and others who were Gentiles, but who have both been brought into the new creation by a second birth and united to the Lord Himself by the Spirit, thus becoming one Body with Him and each other. It was this great truth that Paul was specially called to minister "according to the gift of the grace of God," which had been bestowed upon him. The Holy Spirit effectually worked in and through him to bring lost sinners of the Gentiles into this wonderful place of privilege and inalienable blessing.

Note how meekly the apostle speaks of himself, even in connection with this great ministry committed to him, which was enough to have turned any ordinary man's head. He says, "Unto me, who am less than the least of all saints, is this grace given." He was not exalted by the abundance of the revelation made known to him, but accepted it as a divine trust which he was to minister for the glory of God and the blessing of others. Alas, what a different spirit often actuates some today, who, getting a little smattering of truth, are carried away by their fancied superior intelligence, and manifest the most shocking pride and conceit because of the imagined inferiority of other believers who have not yet attained to their knowledge of the truth! Surely every new divine revelation to our souls should only humble us the more as we realize that we have nothing that we have not received. Apart from divine grace, we would still be in nature's darkness and ignorance. Paul took the very lowest place as he went about preaching among the Gentiles the unsearchable riches of Christ. To those who were in the greatest spiritual poverty he proclaimed the possibilities of wealth beyond the power of human tongue to express, and he would have all men enter into the blessedness of this, and enjoy in reality the fellowship of the mystery, or, as we might render it, the communion of this secret. Men form their secret societies and delight to meet in hidden places to enjoy together mysteries that others cannot share. The Christian is through grace already a mem-

ber of the society of the redeemed, a fellowship
divinely formed by the indwelling of the Holy
Spirit, and as such can enjoy with fellow-believers the marvelous secret which God has now made
known. From the beginning of the world it has
been hidden in Himself, He who created all
things by Jesus Christ. Observe, it was not simply hidden in the Bible, as though the Old Testament contained this message and we only needed
to ferret it out. But it was hidden in God, and
could not have been apprehended by man at all
excepting by divine revelation. Upon the rejection
of the Lord Jesus Christ by Israel, and the de-
scent of the Holy Spirit to bear witness to the
perfection of His finished work, it pleased God to
make known this mystery. Even angels, whether
good or bad, had no knowledge of it until it was
given to God's saints on earth. This, I understand, is what is involved in the remarkable statement of verse 10, "To the intent that now unto
the principalities and powers in heavenly places
might be known by (or really, through) the
Church, the manifold wisdom of God." That is,
the unseen hosts of glorious beings in the heavens,
as well as the vast armies of fallen spirits dominated by Satan, are learning, as they observe
what God is doing here on earth in His Church,
the many-sided wisdom of God, "according to the
purpose of the ages, which He purposed in Christ
Jesus our Lord." One of our poets has written:

"Through the ages
One unceasing purpose runs."

The humble student of the Word of God can see unfolded in the New Testament the great purpose that God had in mind, when He created the universe and man and counseled with Himself to take out of that world from the children of Adam a vast company who would be united to His blessed Son throughout eternity. All will work out for the glory of Christ Jesus, our Lord.

In Him we now have immediate access with fullest confidence into the presence of God. We are so intimately linked up with Him, so truly one with Him, that we can approach the throne of grace without dread or fear, knowing that all we ask in His name, that is, by His authority, the Father delights to do.

No wonder the apostle could glory in suffering because of this great truth, and he would not have the saints become discouraged because of his trials, but he rather would have them remember that whatever tribulation he was passing through was on their behalf and for their glory.

To the extent that we enter into and appropriate these precious things for ourselves, will be our practical sanctification—our separation from the world and worldly-religious systems that ignore entirely the truth of the mystery of the one Body. He who thus apprehends his unity with

Christ, and hence with all who are in Christ, cannot be sectarian in heart or practice, but must of very necessity embrace all believers in his fellowship and interest.

To profess to hold the truth of the one Body is one thing. To be held by it is quite another. It is an amazing thing to realize that so intimate is the link that binds all believers to each other and to our glorified Head in heaven that everything I say or do as a Christian has an effect for good or ill on all my fellow-members, just as every part of the human body affects every other part. How careful this should make us in our walk and our attitude toward one another.

LECTURE XIII.

PAUL'S SECOND PRAYER FOR THE SAINTS

✦ ✦ ✦

"For this cause I bow my knees unto the Father of our Lord Jesus Christ, of whom the whole family in heaven and earth is named, that He would grant you, according to the riches of His glory, to be strengthened with might by His Spirit in the inner man; that Christ may dwell in your hearts by faith; that ye, being rooted and grounded in love, may be able to comprehend with all saints what is the breadth, and length, and depth, and height; and to know the love of Christ, which passeth knowledge, that ye might be filled with all the fulness of God. Now unto Him that is able to do exceeding abundantly above all that we ask or think, according to the power that worketh in us, unto Him be glory in the Church by Christ Jesus throughout all ages, world without end. Amen" (Eph. 3: 14-21).

✦ ✦ ✦

WE have two prayers in this precious epistle. In the first chapter we have the prayer for knowledge, and in the third, the prayer for love. After reading the first prayer we naturally find ourselves looking out over the great sphere of God's eternal purpose, trying to take in the scope of His wonderful prearranged divine plan. But, as we read the second prayer and meditate upon it, we find ourselves

looking up in adoring gratitude, with our hearts
going out in love to the One who first loved us.

As we try to expound this prayer I want you to
think of seven words that I believe will help us
to get its scope. We read in verse 14, "For this
cause I bow my knees unto the Father of our
Lord Jesus Christ." The expression, "I bow my
knees," is a very beautiful one and suggests intensity of feeling. Have you ever noticed that if
you are just quietly engaged in prayer or meditation, you may sit, perhaps, as I often do, in a
comfortable big chair with your open Bible before
you, and as one thought or another comes, you
close your eyes and lift your heart to God in
prayer? Or, when you come together with God's
people, you love to stand in holy silence before
God joining with some one who is leading in
prayer. But when you are intensely in earnest,
when something has fairly gripped you that stirs
you to deepest supplication, you find yourself almost irresistibly forced to your knees.

"For this cause—" For what cause? Because
of his deep interest in the people of God, because
of his desire that they should enter fully into
their privileges in Christ, and understand the
great mystery of which he had spoken. "For this
cause I bow my knees unto the Father of our
Lord Jesus Christ." We noticed that the first
prayer is addressed to the God of our Lord Jesus
Christ, for God as such is the Source of all coun-

sels, but this second prayer, which has to do more with family relationship, is addressed to the Father of our Lord Jesus Christ. Divine titles are used most discriminately in the Word of God; never in the careless way that we so often use them. We might not think it made any difference whether one said, "I address myself to the God of our Lord Jesus," or, "I bow my knees to the Father of our Lord Jesus," but it made a great deal of difference to the apostle. It indicated the different thoughts that were in his mind.

When I think of God, I think of the Maker of all things, the Planner of all things who fitted the ages together. But I think of the Father as the One from whose bosom the eternal Son came into this world, becoming Man for our salvation. Ere He left this scene He said to Mary, "I ascend unto My Father, and your Father; and to My God, and your God" (John 20:17). There, you see, you have the two thoughts: God the Source of all counsels; the Father, the Source of all affections —family affection, the very center of family relationship.

"I bow my knees unto the Father of our Lord Jesus Christ, of whom the whole family in heaven and earth is named." "The whole family" is undoubtedly a correct rendering here, and yet "every family" would be just as correct, and you probably will want to ask yourself the question:

"What conveys to my mind the most precious thought?" "The whole family"—that means that all saints in earth and heaven constitute one great family of born again ones, and are thus linked up with the Father. But I am thinking, too, of the great hosts of angels never redeemed by the blood of Christ because they have never fallen, and even those who fell found no Saviour. The angels, too, own the Fatherhood of God, but they are servants, waiting on the family. And then there is the family of the Old Testament saints. There was the antediluvian family, the patriarchal family, the Israelites, those who were truly of Israel. All these were families through the past dispensations. And then there is the Church of this age of grace, and by-and-by there will be the glorious kingdom family. There are dispensational distinctions, but all receive life from the same blessed Person, and all together adore and worship Him. Notice that the whole family is located in heaven and on earth. Those who are dead to us are living to God above.

Now you have the prayer proper. First there is our *endowment*. "That He would grant you, according to the riches of His glory." You may come to God in prayer for anything, and realize that since you have such a marvelous endowment as that, you do not need to fear to present your petitions to God. You cannot ask too much. You remember the man who came to a king asking for something, and the king gave to him out of his abundant treasure until the suppliant said, "Your Majesty, that is too much! That is too much!" The king smiled and said, "It may seem too much for you to take, but it is not too much for me to give." And so our blessed God gives out of His abundance. "Able to do exceeding abundantly above all that we ask or think." He does not say, as we sometimes think, "Able to do exceeding abundantly above all that we *can* ask or think," for we could be like little children asking for the moon, but he says that He does for us, "exceeding abundantly above all that we ask or think." When we come to Him in the name of Jesus, bringing our petitions, there is more in that great endowment fund than we can ever exhaust.

"According to the riches of His glory." "According to," not "out of the riches of His glory." We have noticed the difference between these two expressions when commenting on a similar passage found in chapter one, so we need not repeat the illustration we used then. But it means much to the soul when one truly sees this distinction.

Then observe the next phrase. We have in it, our *enduement*. "To be strengthened with might by His Spirit in the inner man." Do you sometimes feel your limitations, your weakness, your lack of intensity of purpose, your powerlessness

when it comes to living for God and witnessing
for Him? Do you feel as though you might as
well give up for the little you accomplish? Do
you say, "If I only had more strength, how different it might be"? Listen! The excellency of the
power is of God, not of us, and the Holy Spirit
who dwells within us is ready to work in and
through us to the glory of our Lord Jesus Christ.
So the prayer is that we may be "strengthened
with might by His Spirit in the inner man." You
know we are not walking storage-batteries. Some
people have an idea that this is practically what
the Christian should be. You hear people pray,
"O God, give me more power, fill me with power."
The idea they have is that the old battery is
pretty well run down. "Put another one in, Lord,"
is what they seem to say. No, you are not a
storage-battery; you are in connection with the
great eternal dynamo, and the Holy Spirit works
in and through you to the glory of the Lord Jesus
Christ as you are yielded to Him. He Himself is
the source of all power, and that power is to be
used by the people of God.

The next word is *enthronement.* "That Christ
may dwell in your hearts by faith." Is this not
the same thing as when in another epistle He
speaks of Christ reigning? Is it not Christ sitting
upon the throne of our hearts dominating, con-
trolling us for the glory of God, His blessed
pierced hands guiding and directing everything?

It is not Christ received as an occasional visitor, not Christ recognized merely as a guest, but Christ abiding within as our living, loving, blessed Lord: Christ dwelling in the heart by faith. You remember the little couplet,

> "If Christ is not Lord of all,
> He is not Lord at all."

He does not want the second place. He must have the first if your life is going to be that which it should.

The next thing is our *establishment*. "That ye, being rooted and grounded in love." He uses a figure here that you will find in other of his epistles, "rooted and grounded." The two terms are very different. When I was a boy, the school-teacher used to tell me that I must not mix my metaphors. For instance, I should not start with the figure of a ship and change to that of a rail-road in the same sentence. But the Holy Ghost is wonderfully independent in His use of metaphors. "That ye, being rooted and grounded in love." Rooted like a tree, and grounded like a building which is raised upon a great foundation. Rooted and grounded in what? In love. What is love? That is the great rock foundation upon which we build, for God is love, and he who is rooted in love is rooted in God, and therefore, the right-eous shall flourish like the palm tree. The believer is like the trees, for they draw their nourishment from the living God Himself. What a Christian character will be built when one is founded upon this Rock, building upon God Himself, rooted and grounded in love!

And now we have our *enlightenment*. "That ye may be able to comprehend with all saints." You will never be able to take it all in, but you comprehend a little, and another a little, and I a little, and with all the saints together we begin to get some idea of God's wonderful purpose of grace. Therefore, we need one another, we need fellowship, we need to be helpers of each other's faith. The feeblest, the weakest member of the Body of Christ is necessary, for God may give to some feeble crippled brother what some strong active Christian may never get at all. "That ye may be able to comprehend with all saints what is the breadth, and length, and depth, and height." Of what? Some say of love. What has He been speaking about in this chapter? God's wonderful purpose of the ages, God's great plan. It is that by the Spirit you may be able to comprehend with all saints what is the breadth, and length, and depth, and height of that vast system of grace which God is working out through the ages of time and which will be consummated in the ages to come.

In school I was told that no solid could have more than three dimensions, length, breadth, and thickness; but we have here length, breadth,

depth, and height—four dimensions. Could you
draw a picture of this? Could you draw an illustration of length, breadth, depth, and height?
How would you do it? Some of the old Greek
philosophers used to reason about a possible
fourth dimension, and with them it was a kind
of weird spiritual dimension. After all, that is
not so bad. You remember that Spanish prisoner
whose bones were discovered when Napoleon's
soldiers opened the prison of the Inquisition.
There in an underground dungeon they found the
skeleton of the prisoner, flesh and clothing all
long since gone, but the remnants of an ankle bone
with a chain attached to it were still there. There
upon the wall they saw cut into the rock with a
sharp piece of metal a cross, and above it in
Spanish, the word for height, and below it the
word for depth, and on one arm the word for
for length, and on the other the word for breadth.
As that poor prisoner of so long ago was starving
to death, his soul was contemplating the wonder
of God's purpose of grace, and to Him the figure
of the cross summed it all up — the length, the
breadth, the depth, the height!

Next he prays that we may "know the love of
Christ which passeth knowledge." Surely this is
our *enlargement*. We glory as we enter into the
knowledge of the love of Christ; but what a
strange expression is this! He prays that we
may know the unknowable. "The love of Christ

that passeth knowledge." See that darling little babe in the mother's arms, looking up and cooing and responding to the mother's smile. You or I might say, "Let me take the little one," and hold out our hands, and it would look at us and cling the more tightly to the mother, and if we should insist on taking it, it might utter a piercing cry which would say, "I do not know you; I do not know whether you love babies or not, but I know my mother's love and can trust her." And yet, what does the baby know of the love of a mother? What does it understand about the reasons behind a mother's love? But it enjoys it nevertheless. And so the youngest saint in Christ knows the love of the Saviour, and the oldest saint, the most mature saint, is still seeking to know in greater fulness that love that passeth knowledge.

> "Oh, the love of Christ is boundless,
>   Broad and long and deep and high!
> Every doubt and fear is groundless,
>   Now the Word of faith is nigh.
> Jesus Christ for our salvation,
>   Came and shed His precious blood;
> Clear we stand from condemnation,
>   In the risen Son of God."

Then notice the last point in this prayer, "That ye might be filled with all the fulness of God." Or properly, "That ye might be filled unto all the fulness of God." This is our *enrichment*. When our translators said, "Filled with all the fulness of God," they meant well, but you could not hold all the fulness of God. Solomon said, "Even the heaven of heavens cannot contain Thee." Yet we read that He dwells in the heart of him that is humble and contrite. Walking by the seaside one time, some one touched the real meaning of this word. He picked up one of the beautiful sea-shells and put it down in the sand where the water had ebbed for a moment or two, and then as they watched, the sea came rolling in and the shell was filled, and he said, "See! Filled unto all the fulness of the ocean." So you and I as we live in fellowship with God may be filled unto His fulness. We are in Him and He is in us, and thus the prayer is answered.

And now notice the closing wonderful benediction. "Now unto Him that is able to do above all we ask"; is that what is written? No; that is not enough. Is it, "Able to do abundantly above all that we ask"? That is not enough. Is it, "Able to do exceeding abundantly above all that we ask?" Still that does not reach the limit. "Unto Him that is able to do exceeding abundantly above all that we ask or think." You need not fear to come to God about anything. Are you troubled about present circumstances? Have you availed yourself of the abundant resources of God? If things are right in your heart and you come to God and make connections there, you can be sure of a wonderful answer. "Unto Him that is able to do exceeding abundantly above all that we ask or think, according to the power that worketh in us"—this divine energy which works through poor feeble creatures such as we are— "Unto Him be glory in the Church by Christ Jesus throughout all ages, world without end. Amen." He is the One in whom God will find His pleasure throughout all eternity.

THE WALK WORTHY OF
OUR CALLING

� ✻ ✻

"I therefore, the prisoner of the Lord, beseech you that
ye walk worthy of the vocation wherewith ye are called.
With all lowliness and meekness, with longsuffering, forbearing one another in love; endeavoring to keep the unity
of the Spirit in the bond of peace. There is one Body, and
one Spirit, even as ye are called in one hope of your calling: one Lord, one faith, one baptism, one God and Father
of all, who is above all, and through all, and in you all"
(Eph. 4: 1-6).

✻ ✻ ✻

IN chapters one to three we have been studying
the doctrinal section of this letter to the
Ephesians. We now take up the practical
part, that which has to do with our lives as those
who through grace have been made members of
Christ. Notice how tenderly the apostle leads us
to this. He says, "I therefore, the prisoner of the
Lord, beseech you that ye walk worthy of the
vocation wherewith ye are called."

Wherever grace rules in the soul, "I command"
is changed to "I beseech." You do not find the
apostle lording it over the faith of the people of
God, but graciously, tenderly pleading with them,

rather than sternly ordering their behavior. He speaks of himself in a way that certainly must have gone home to the heart of every one who read this letter in its original setting, for these Ephesians had been brought to know the Saviour's love through him, and the link between a preacher and those who have been brought to Christ as a result of his ministry is a very real one. Hearts are very closely bound together when they stand in that relationship. What must they have felt to realize that the man of God to whom they owed so much was lying in a Roman prison, and he was there not because of any ill-doing on his part, but because of his faithful proclamation of the gospel which had meant so much to them. He was a prisoner of the Lord, and from his prison-cell he writes this letter, beseeching them to walk worthy of the vocation wherewith they are called.

Our vocation is, of course, our calling. Paul refers to that which he has been previously opening up in these other chapters. He has been putting before us the blessedness of the new life, that all who believe on the Lord Jesus Christ are members of that one Body of which He is the exalted Head in heaven, and that all such have been builded together for a habitation of God by the Spirit. In view of the fact that we have been redeemed to God by the precious blood of Christ; in view of the fact that I am a member now of His body, of His flesh, and of His bones; in view of the fact that I am a living stone built into that temple of God by the Holy Spirit, that temple in which He dwells, my behavior is to be ordered of God, I am to walk worthy of the vocation wherewith I am called. Elsewhere we are told to walk worthy of God and of the Lord.

"With all lowliness and meekness, with longsuffering, forbearing one another in love." I spent quite a little time over this verse. It went home to my own heart, for every expression in it was a challenge to me, and I kept asking myself the question, "To what extent have I risen to the standard that is here set forth? I must present this to others as the divine standard for a Christian's behavior. To what extent am I measuring up to it?" And the more I carefully examined every expression both in the English and in the original Greek, the more humiliated and ashamed before God I was as I realized how far short I have often come—I am afraid, I always come—from living out what we have here. Every word is important.

"With all lowliness." That word is found only once elsewhere in the New Testament and that is in the Epistle to the Philippians, chapter 2:3. "Let nothing be done through strife or vainglory; but in lowliness of mind let each esteem other better than themselves." The original word means "modesty," that is, an utter lack of self-assertiveness, that which is so characteristic of us as fallen creatures—we who have nothing to be proud of and yet are sometimes proud of our very crudity and ignorance. A young minister arose in a Methodist Conference and said, "I am against education. I don't believe in education. I read no books except the Bible; I don't profess to know nothing about literature or anything of that kind; I am just an ignorant man. But the Lord has taken me up, and is using me, and I am not at all interested in schools or colleges or education. I am proud to be just what I am." An old preacher arose and said, "Do I understand that our dear young brother is proud of his ignorance? If so, all I have to say is that he has a great deal to be proud of." Most of us are that way; we are proud of the very thing of which we ought to be ashamed. We begin to boast of our attainments and ability, even as children. One of the first things parents must learn in training their children is to curb that natural tendency to boastfulness. But as Christians, how completely we should be delivered from this. We have nothing that we have not received. Every blessing we have we owe to divine grace. With what modesty, then, should we behave ourselves!

The word "meekness" is found eight times in the New Testament. I should like, if there were time, to turn to every one of the passages, but I would remind you of this, that it is used of our blessed Lord Himself. The apostle says, "We beseech you by the meekness and gentleness of Christ," and Christ says, "Take My yoke upon you, and learn of Me; for I am meek and lowly in heart: and ye shall find rest unto your souls" (Matt. 11: 29). The root of the original word really means "humility," a spirit that never takes offence. Somebody says something unkind about me. I flare up in a moment. Why? Because I am not meek. They said of Jesus, "He has a devil," and He meekly endured it. They said, "Say we not right that Thou art a Samaritan?" But He answered them not. "When He was reviled, He reviled not again; when He suffered, He threatened not." That is meekness.

And then the next word, "longsuffering." This is a favorite word of the apostle, and we also find it used twice by the Apostle Peter. It is found twelve times in the New Testament. It means literally, "to endure with unruffled temper." Do you know very much about longsuffering? "Well," you say, "I would not mind if what she said about me had been true, but when I know it isn't true, I can't stand it." Therefore, the need of long-suffering. It is the flesh which talks like that. That does not come from the new nature but from the old. Many years ago I had a friend, a little, odd German brother, whose name was George. Sometimes he would fly off and lose his temper, but it always brought him back to earth if one looked at him quietly and said, "Is that old George

or new George talking?" In a moment the tears
would come; and even now, though he has been
gone thirty years, I can hear him say, "That's
old George; new George would neffer behafe that
way. I must take that old George and inflict
punishment upon him. He has no right to behafe
like that." Yes, the old nature is quick to take
offence, quick to flare up if not properly appre-
ciated, but the new nature just bows in meekness
and lets the waves and billows pass over and is
undisturbed thereby.

The last word here is "forbearing." "Forbearing one another in love." This word occurs
only once otherwise in the New Testament and
that is in Colossians 3 : 13. There we have a very
similar expression to that which is before us here:
"Forbearing one another, and forgiving one another, if any man have a quarrel against any:
even as Christ forgave you, so also do ye." Literally, forbearance means "to put up with." Now
taking all that into account I thought I would try
to translate that verse myself. I am going to give
you the Authorized Version first, and then my
own translation. "With all lowliness and meekness, with longsuffering, forbearing one another
in love." My translation is, "With all modesty
and humbleness of spirit, with unruffled temper,
lovingly putting up with all that is disagreeable
in other people." That is a literal rendering of
the original. That is the Spirit of Christ. As we

meditate upon it and think of all that is involved in it, how can we do other than hang our heads in shame and confess that in many things we all offend, but seek grace that we may be so yielded to the control of the Holy Spirit of God that these things may indeed become real in our lives?

The apostle goes on, "Endeavoring to keep the unity of the Spirit in the bond of peace." Others have translated it, "Giving diligence to keep the unity of the Spirit in the bond of peace." Observe, he does not say, "Giving diligence to keep the unity of the Body." We do not have anything to do with that. We do not have to preserve the unity of the Body. God is looking after that. He has bound every believer up in a bundle in Christ, has given His blessed Holy Spirit to dwell within, and He links them one to another, and to the blessed Head in heaven. The Body of Christ is always complete as God looks at it. People talk about "these heartless divisions that rend the Body of Christ," but they do not rend the Body of Christ. You see, the Body of Christ is not composed of all the different sects and denominations. If you were to gather all the different Catholic sects together, the Roman Catholic, the Greek Catholic, the Chaldean Catholic, the Anglican Catholic, the Coptic Catholic, etc., and then gather all the Protestant sects together and unite them all in one big church, that would not be the Body of Christ. That would contain a great many people who are in the Body of Christ but it would also include a great many who are not. On the other hand, after you had gathered all these denominations and sects together, there would be a great many outside that would be members of the Body of Christ, for "The Church, which is His Body," and the Church, which some call the visible Body of Christ, are not the same thing. The Body of Christ consists only of those who are regenerated and born again by the Holy Spirit and linked to Christ in glory by the Spirit's baptism, and all the divisions in Christendom cannot rend that Body. But what have they done? They certainly have denied the unity of the Spirit. The apostle would have us recognize this unity which God Himself has constituted, and so he says, "Endeavoring to keep the unity of the Spirit in the bond of peace."

The Spirit unites us to that Body which He has formed, and now He says, "I want you to recognize it." When you meet with fellow-believers, do you endeavor to keep the unity of the Spirit, do you realize that you belong to them and they belong to you? "But," you say, "they do not see things the way I do." If they belong to Christ, they belong to you and you to them. We are to do this in the uniting bond of peace. Some years ago I was taken ill in the midst of a series of meetings at Minneapolis. After my fourth address I went out one Sunday noon to take dinner, and

right after the meal I tumbled over, and when I
regained consciousness I had a fever of one hundred and two degrees and was ill with typhoid. I
was down for six weeks. As soon as I had
strength enough to start home my friends helped
me to the station. I could not walk alone, but
they assisted me, and the porter was very court-
eous. He made up a berth and put both mat-
tresses on, and let me recline there all day long.
The first morning as I lay there with a lot of
pillows behind me, I took out my Bible and was
getting my morning portion. Of course you never
start the day without at least a little portion from
the Word of God; do you? You do? Well, that
is why you have so many bad days. I was reading from the Word of God when a rather stout-
looking German lady came walking by, and she
stopped and said, "Vat's dat? A Bible?" I said,
"Yes." "Vell, you haf your morning worship all
by yourself? Vait," she said, "I go get my Bible
and we haf it together." She came back and settled herself on my couch and said, "Var are you
reading?" A little later a tall gentleman came by,
and stopped and said, "Reading the Bible! Vell,
I tank I go get mine, too." He was a Norwegian,
and he came back with his Bible, and in a few
minutes I was amazed at the people who crowded
around. They did the same thing every day, and
we had a delightful time all the way to California.
I would get my Bible, and then they would begin

to come, and sometimes there would be as many as twenty-eight Bibles. The conductor would go all through the cars and say, "The camp-meeting is beginning in car number so-and-so. Any wanting to take advantage are invited." They sometimes got so full they would start a hymn, sometimes we would have a little prayer, and sometimes it would be only the Bible reading, and they would ask questions. That went on until we reached Sacramento, where some of the cars were to be cut off and go down the valley. So the people from the other cars came in to say good-bye, and this dear German sister came and said, "Oh, it has been just like a camp-meeting all the way. It has fed my soul. I am going to Turlock, but I want to ask you, What denomination are you?"

"Well," I said, "I belong to the same denomination that David did."

"What was that? I didn't know that David belonged to any."

"David said, 'I am a companion of all them that fear Thee and keep Thy precepts.'"

"Yah, yah," she said; "that is a good church to belong to."

Why, dear friends, I suppose if we had interrogated those people, we would have found that we belonged to a dozen different sects, but the blessed thing was, we found we were all one in Christ. Oh, that we might "endeavor to keep the unity of the Spirit in the bond of peace," not in contentiousness, not in quarreling, but all alike seeking to glorify the Lord Jesus Christ, our Saviour.

In the last three verses the apostle brings before us a sevenfold unity. Notice; "There is one Body, and one Spirit, even as ye are called in one hope of your calling; one Lord, one faith, one baptism, one God and Father of all, who is above all, and through all, and in you all." Seven different unities all linked up in one. One great confession, and yet it is easy to see that there are three distinct spheres indicated, becoming larger and larger. Verse four speaks of that unity which is absolutely vital, "There is one Body." That is the Body of Christ, and, as we have seen, that Body is composed only of people who have been washed from their sins in the blood of our Lord Jesus Christ, regenerated by the Word and by the Spirit, and thus made members of Christ. Then in the second place, "There is one Spirit," and this is the one Holy Spirit by whose operation we have been baptized into the Body of Christ. We read in 1 Corinthians 12: 13, "For by one Spirit are we all baptized into one Body, whether we be bond or free; and have been all made to drink into one Spirit." "One Body, and one Spirit," and then, "one hope"—"Even as ye are called in one hope of your calling." All believers have the same blessed hope, the hope of some day, some day soon, beholding the face of our Lord Jesus

Christ and being transformed into His image. All real believers are included here—one Body, one Spirit, one hope of your calling.

But now the second sphere is a little bit wider. It does not necessarily include only those who are born again. It may include those who have made a profession which is not real. "One Lord, one faith, one baptism." You see, there are those who say, "Lord, Lord," who have never been born again. Jesus says that in the day of judgment many shall come to Him and say, "Lord, Lord, have we not prophesied in Thy name? and in Thy name have cast out devils? and in Thy name have done many wonderful works? And then will I profess unto them, I never knew you: depart from Me, ye that work iniquity." Take, for instance, the part of the world which we speak of as Christendom. What do people write at the head of their letters? They write 1936.* And what does that mean? It means, in the year of our Lord 1936. I suppose every racketeer and gangster in Chicago dates his letters that way. "Why call ye Me, Lord, Lord, and do not the things which I say?" (Luke 6:46). There are lots of hypocrites in Christendom who call Him Lord, and yet show by their lives that they have never been born again.

---

*This lecture was delivered in 1936.

Then there is the one faith. This is not the faith by which we are saved, but the faith of the Christian Church, the faith which was once for all delivered to the saints. It is the one standard of truth that God has given to be proclaimed in the world, it is that which the apostle calls *the faith*. Faith in Christ is confidence in Jesus, but *the* faith is the body of the Christian doctrine.

Then there is baptism, the outward expression of allegiance to Christ. Some say, "Do you think that baptism here is water baptism, or the baptism of the Spirit?" I say without a moment's hesitation, "Water baptism," for we have seven unities. We have already had the baptism of the Spirit, "one Body, one Spirit," and we do not have the Spirit repeated here. If it were the baptism of the Spirit, you would have only a sixfold unity, but baptism is the outward expression of allegiance to Christ. A man may profess to belong to Christ and be baptized, but that does not prove he is really born again. The mark of Christ has been put upon some men and yet they have never truly received Him into their hearts. What a solemn thing this is! I wonder if any of you are in the wider circle, you have never been born again, you are not in the first circle but are among those who have made profession, whether real or not, and, therefore, are in the second circle. Can it be that you have made a profession of Christ, that the mark of Christ has been put upon you, that you have been baptized in the name of the Father and of the Son and of the Holy Ghost, and yet have never trusted Christ? What an awful thing for a lost one in the pit of woe to have to say, "I bore Christ's mark on earth; I was baptized in recognition of His death and suffering, and yet here I am lost for all eternity because I did not trust that Saviour who suffered for me."

Notice the third circle. This is very much wider than the others, for it takes in God's relationship to the entire creation. "One God," and as such He is in relationship to all His creatures, "and Father of all, who is above all, and through all, and in you all." This is not the modern doctrine of the universal Fatherhood of God and the universal brotherhood of man, but it means that God is the Creator of all men. "One God and Father of all, who is above all, and through all, and in you all." He is a distinct Personality. This is not pantheism, not God as a principle, but God, a divine Personality, and yet immanent in grace, not far from any one of us.

He is the living God, the divine Personality, the transcendent God, God over all, pre-eminent, directing all things, pervading everything. He is "in you all." That is the distinction between God's attitude toward the world as a whole and toward those who have been born again—"in you all." If you have accepted Christ, if you have trusted Him, God dwells in you. What a wonderful truth, what a marvelous thing this is! He says, "I will dwell in them, I will walk in them." As we walk the streets we can realize that God is walking with us, and so we may well come back to the exhortation with which we began, "Walk worthy of the vocation wherewith ye are called."

GIFTS FROM THE ASCENDED CHRIST

✓ ✓ ✓

"But unto every one of us is given grace according to the measure of the gift of Christ. Wherefore He saith, When He ascended up on high, He led captivity captive, and gave gifts unto men. (Now that He ascended, what is it but that He also descended first into the lower parts of the earth? He that descended is the same also that ascended up far above all heavens, that He might fill all things.) And He gave some, apostles; and some, prophets; and some, evangelists; and some, pastors and teachers; for the perfecting of the saints, for the work of the ministry, for the edifying of the Body of Christ: till we all come in the unity of the faith, and of the knowledge of the Son of God, unto a perfect man, unto the measure of the stature of the fulness of Christ" (Eph. 4:7-13).

✓ ✓ ✓

OUR attention in these verses is especially drawn to the gifts that the ascended Christ has bestowed upon His Church for its edification, its upbuilding. First observe that there are gifts for all—"Unto every one of us is given grace according to the measure of the gift of Christ." While there are certain outstanding gifts of what we might call a public character, yet it is blessed to realize that every member of the Body of Christ has something which he may con-

tribute to the blessing of the whole. No matter
how feeble, how insignificant, how relatively unknown he may be, he has received something from
the risen Lord for the help of all the rest.

Just as there are many members of our physical bodies that are unseen, which function without any outward evidence of their working, and
yet are very important in connection with the
building of the body and the maintaining of it in
health, so every believer has his place to fill in
the Body of Christ. If he is not functioning according to the will of God, in some respect he
affects the whole body for ill, but if he is functioning according to the will of God he affects the
entire Body of Christ for good. These gifts come
from the ascended Lord.

In verse 8 we read, "Wherefore He saith, When
He ascended up on high, He led captivity captive,
and gave gifts unto men." Our blessed Lord
chose apostles when He was here on earth, but
said that in the regeneration, that is, in the
glorious Millennial age, they should sit on thrones
judging the twelve tribes of Israel. As the
ascended Christ He has given apostles and prophets to His Church, but they are given from
heaven. They included the same apostles that He
chose on earth, but it was after their enduement
with the Holy Spirit at Pentecost, the Spirit that
He Himself sent, that they were looked upon as
given to the Church.

The passage here is quoted from Psalm 68:
"Thou hast ascended on high, Thou hast led captivity captive." Just what is meant by that rather
peculiar expression? It is a Hebraism. It is
taken over literally from the Hebrew. Psalm 68:
18 reads: "Thou hast ascended on high, Thou hast
led captivity captive: Thou hast received gifts for
men: yea, for the rebellious also, that the Lord
God might dwell among them." In the margin
of our Authorized Version we have the suggestion
that the expression, "Captivity captive," in Eph.
4, might be rendered, "a multitude of captives."
That is an attempt to explain a rather peculiar
phrase, but when we realize that this is simply
a translation of an expression in the psalm, we
have to inquire whether the Hebrew text could
be translated, "A multitude of captives." I think
any Hebrew scholar would acknowledge that it
could not. And that is not the only place where
this expression is found.

In Judges 5 you have the same expression.
Deborah is praising the Lord for the great victory
over Canaan. In verse 12 we read, "Awake,
awake, Deborah: awake, utter a song: arise,
Barak, and lead thy captivity captive, thou son of
Abinoam." What does the expression mean there?
It could mean only one thing—"Lead captive him
who held you captive." That seems to be the
meaning of Ps. 68:18, and also of this quotation
in the Epistle to the Ephesians.

In Isaiah 14 we have a similar expression which would be an adequate interpretation of the term. We read, "And the people shall take them, and bring them to their place: and the house of Israel shall possess them in the land of the Lord for servants and handmaids: and they shall take them captives, whose captives they were; and they shall rule over their oppressors" (Isa. 14:2). This surely makes the meaning clear. In our present passage the teaching is this, that our blessed Lord in His triumph over death led captive him who had the power of death up to that time, that He might deliver those "who through fear of death were all their lifetime subject to bondage" (Heb. 2:15). In other words, our mighty enemy, Satan, is now a conquered foe. He has been led captive at the chariot-wheels of Christ, and our Lord has now ascended as Man and taken His place upon the throne of the Majesty in the heavens, and there from His exalted seat in glory He gives these gifts to His Church for its edification and blessing. We are reminded that He who has gone up higher than any other man ever went, once for our redemption went down lower than any other man has gone.

"Now that He ascended, what is it but that He also descended first into the lower parts of the earth? He that descended is the same also that ascended up far above all heavens, that He might

fill all things." I wonder if our souls really take
in the fact that He is a Man like ourselves, only
glorified, sinless, and holy, sitting today upon the
throne of God, that a man's heart beats in His
breast, and that there are no sorrows that
come to His people but what He enters sympathetically, compassionately, into them, and therefore, having "not an high priest which cannot be
touched with the feeling of our infirmities, but
was in all points tempted like as we are," we may
"come boldly unto the throne of grace, that we
may obtain mercy, and find grace to help in time
of need" (Heb. 4: 15, 16).

"There's a Man in the glory I know very well,
 I have known Him for years, and His goodness can tell;
 One day in His mercy He knocked at my door,
 And asking admittance knocked many times o'er;
 But when I went to Him and stood face to face
 And listened a while to His story of grace,
 How He suffered for sinners and put away sin,
 I heartily, thankfully, welcomed Him in."

And now I have the blessed assurance from the
Word of God that that Man sits there at the
Father's right hand ever living to make intercession for His needy people as they go through this
scene.

Go to Him in the hour of trial, "tell not half
the story, but the whole," and be assured that He
will listen sympathetically and undertake for you
according to the riches of His grace. He always

has undertaken for His people in a marvelous way.

"He gave some, apostles; and some, prophets; and some, evangelists; and some, pastors and teachers; for the perfecting of the saints, for the work of the ministry, for the edifying of the Body of Christ." These are the gifts that Christ Himself has given. We have in 1 Cor. 12 special operations of the Holy Spirit which were for the Church in the beginning of its early conflict with heathenism, and in giving its chief testimony to Judaism. But here the gifts are for the edification, for the maintenance of the Church, given by the risen Christ to enable the Church to carry the message to a lost world, and to build up its individual members in the knowledge of Christ. The apostles and prophets laid the foundation. We read in Eph. 2:20: "And are built upon the foundation of the apostles and prophets, Jesus Christ Himself being the chief corner stone." You do not lay a foundation for a building every few stories, but the foundation is built once for all, and then the superstructure is erected. Long ago, nineteen hundred years ago, the apostles and prophets fulfilled their ministry. We are not looking for new apostles and prophets.

A young Mormon elder came to me at one time and asked, "What church do you belong to?" I knew at once what he had in mind, and so I replied, "I belong to the one true Church that has apostles and prophets in it."

"Oh," he said, "then you must be a latter-day saint."

"No, I am a former-day saint."

"But ours is the only church that has apostles and prophets."

"I do not think so. The Church that I belong to is building upon the foundation of the apostles and prophets, and although they themselves have passed off the scene long ago they are still members of this Church, for it does not exist only on earth. They are part of the host though they have passed the flood and are in the presence of God. They are still members of the Church."

"But we have apostles and prophets in our day."

"But, you see," I said, "the apostles and prophets were to lay the foundation, and if I understand the Word of God aright, this blessed temple of the living God, this wonderful Church He is erecting, has been building for nineteen hundred years, and it is now just about completed, and you do not put a foundation on the roof. It is away down there nineteen hundred stories below, and the temple has been rising upon that foundation all through the years. We are now just putting the finishing touches on the roof. We are gathering in poor sinners, just one and another here and there. They are not coming in large numbers these days, but those that are coming are being builded in upon the roof, and it will not be long

until it will be complete and then we will all go
to heaven."

And now the other gifts are very manifest today. What is the evangelist? He is the bearer
of glad tidings. The ministry of the evangelist
is particularly to the world outside. If God gifts
a man as an evangelist, He fills his heart with
fervent love for a lost world, gives him the ability
to proclaim the gospel in freshness and power.
What a marvelous gift is that of the evangelist!
We do not all have it in the way we should like
to have it. It is a privilege to try to teach the
Word, to seek to build up the saints, but when I
think of the mighty men that God has qualified
and sent forth as evangelists to win the lost, I
covet such a gift. If you are a young preacher
and have the evangelistic gift, thank God for it,
cherish it, do not despise it. Do not say, "I wish
I could teach the Bible like certain men, exhort
like some of these wonderful men of God, explain
the Scripture in the way that some can." It is
very good if God gifts you for that, but I would
rather be used of God to win poor sinners to
Christ than even to teach and instruct Christians.
Someone at one time reproved old Duncan Mathe-
son for preaching the gospel at a great conference
of believers, and said, "You kept all those people
sitting here for an hour listening to what they
already know, when they came to hear a wonderful unfolding of new truth."

"Why," he said, "were there no sinners here today?"

"Oh, there may have been a few."

"Very well, that is all right then; I did not make a mistake because, you know, if people are Christians, they will manage to wiggle awa' to heaven some way if they never learn another thing, but poor sinners will have to be saved or be in hell."

Never forget that. And if you are a poor sinner today, you are Christless, lost, hopeless. Let me impress it upon you. It must be Christ or hell, and to neglect the one is but to choose the other. I wish I could sound that out in a way that dying men would hear, and hearing would believe and flee from the wrath to come. That is the special province of the evangelist. He goes out into the world and wins souls for Christ, and then the Spirit of God brings them into the Church of God.

And then we read that He gave some, pastors. The word means "shepherds." A true pastor is a shepherd who has a heart for the sheep of Christ's flock. When our blessed Lord challenged Peter with the words, "Lovest thou Me more than these?" and after Peter earnestly confessed, "O Lord, Thou knowest all things, Thou knowest that I love Thee," Jesus said, "Feed My sheep, feed My lambs, shepherd My sheep," and in that He constituted Peter a pastor of His flock. What a

blessed gift that is! The evangelist finds them as
lost sheep wandering in the wilderness and brings
them into the flock, and then the pastor seeks to
lead them into the green pastures of God's Word,
to minister to them when they are sick, to be with
them when they are dying, to point them to the
cross in the hour when faith may be weak, to
enter into their sorrows; and that is what constitutes the work of a real pastor. No theological
seminary, no college or university can make a
pastor. It is the Holy Spirit of God alone who
gives a man a pastor's heart, and fills him with
yearning love for the people of God.

And then the next is that of the teacher. What
is the difference between the pastor and the teacher? In 1 Corinthians 12: 8 we read, "For to one
is given by the Spirit the word of wisdom; to
another the word of knowledge by the same
Spirit." We may say that the pastor has in a
peculiar sense the word of wisdom, the teacher
the word of knowledge. It is the special province
of the teacher to open up the truth of God's Word
in a clear, orderly way so that people may grasp
it and profit by it, that they may understand the
divine plan and thus apply the truth to their own
needs, and it is the responsibility of the pastor to
press the truth home upon the conscience in the
power of the Holy Spirit.

Do you ever remember an experience such as
this? Maybe it was a time in your life when you

were going through some special trial and perplexity, and you said, "I must find my way down
to the place where the people of God are gathered." You entered in with a heavy burden. The
meeting went on, and some one stood up to expound the Word of God, and you were edified.
He took a certain portion of Scripture and made
it clear and beautiful, and it did you good, but
as you left the place you said, "Well, it didn't
touch my case at all. I have no more light upon
my trouble than I had when I came in. I am
glad I came, for I was blessed. I shall always
understand that portion of Scripture better than
I have in the past. It was indeed good to be
there." But you went away with the trouble,
with the burden, with the perplexity. On another
occasion you slipped down again, and this time
some one read a portion of Scripture, and as he
began to expound it you said, "Why, he seems to
know exactly what I am going through. He
seems to understand exactly what my trouble is.
That is just what I need." And as the Word was
unfolded your soul was stirred and your heart
blessed, and you went away saying, "Blessed
Lord, I thank Thee that Thou hast given such
gifts to Thy people; I thank Thee that through
the opening up of Thy truth my perplexity has
been removed." You were listening to the teacher
in the first case, and in the second to the pastor.
One had the word of knowledge and the other the

word of wisdom. What is wisdom? It is knowledge applied to meeting a distinct and definite case.

Look at verse 12. Why did He give apostles, prophets, evangelists, pastors, and teachers? "For the perfecting of the saints, for the work of the ministry, for the edifying of the Body of Christ." Now, just as you have it punctuated in our Authorized Version, what would you understand the work of these special gifts to be? Would you not take it that their ministry was threefold?—that the Lord had given pastors and teachers for three purposes, for the perfecting of the saints, for the work of the ministry, and for the edifying of the Body of Christ? And to what would that conclusion lead you? That the work of perfecting the saints and the work of the ministry and the edifying of the Body belongs entirely to those who have been set apart in a special way as pastors and teachers. That is the conclusion many have come to, and people are quite content to depend upon the man in the pulpit and say, "Don't we engage him to do the work of the ministry? Isn't he to do the work of edifying the Body of Christ?" But there are no punctuation marks in the original text; they have simply been put there by editors. I am going to take the liberty of removing these commas. Go back to verse 11, "He gave some, apostles; and some, prophets; and some evangelists; and some, pastors, and teach-

ers; for the perfecting of the saints for the work
of the ministry for the edifying of the Body of
Christ." Do you see any difference? It is not
that the pastors and teachers are a kind of close
corporation whose business it is to do all these
things. But when God gifts a man as a preacher
or a teacher he is to exercise that gift for the perfecting, the developing, of the saints in order that
they might do the work of the ministry and thus
edify the Body of Christ. This is an altogether
different thing. A dear young fellow came to me
and said, "Are any of your sermons copyrighted?"

"No; indeed they are not," I said.

"I am glad to hear it, because I heard you a
week ago and went out and preached your sermon
at a mission. I wondered whether I had any right
to do it."

I said, "If something gripped your soul that
you can pass on to somebody else and make it a
blessing to them, I thank God for it. If you get
a convert, you will be the father and I will be
the grandfather."

I read in Moody's life story that years ago he
would go on Sunday morning to hear the different preachers of the day, and then in the after-
noon and evening he would be out in the missions
and on the street corners preaching. He would
come back and say to one of these ministers,
"Doctor, I preached your sermon five times last
week, and won about forty souls," and the preach-

er would look at him in a queer way, for he had probably never seen a soul saved for weeks or months. The blessed risen Lord gives some the gift of apostles, some prophets, some evangelists, some pastors, and some teachers, but it is in order that all may profit thereby, for it is for the perfecting of the saints for the work of the ministry and for the edifying of the Body of Christ. Do not be content to come to meeting and just be a spiritual sponge. Fill up, and then let the blessed Lord do some squeezing. Give it out to somebody else, and then you will be carrying out the true principle of New Testament ministry.

How long will this go on? "Till we all come in the unity of the faith, and of the knowledge of the Son of God, unto a perfect man, unto the measure of the stature of the fulness of Christ." What does that mean? It means until at last the entire Church will be gathered home to heaven, and Christ will be fully displayed in every one of us. What is the fulness of Christ? We read in chapter 1: 23: "Which is His Body, the fulness of Him that filleth all in all." Christ is the Head up there in glory, we are the members of His Body and constitute His completeness as the one new man. When at last we have gone home to heaven, our day of toiling over, and we are in all perfection like Himself, then this kind of ministry will be ended. There will be no room for the pastor, for the teacher, for the evangelist in heaven, for there we will all praise alike the name of our blessed Lord Jesus Christ, and none shall need to teach another for all shall know even as we have been known.

MANIFESTING THE TRUTH IN LOVE

✦ ✦ ✦

"That we henceforth be no more children, tossed to and fro, and carried about with every wind of doctrine, by the sleight of men, and cunning craftiness, whereby they lie in wait to deceive; but speaking the truth in love, may grow up into Him in all things, which is the Head, even Christ: from whom the whole Body fitly joined together and compacted by that which every joint supplieth, according to the effectual working in the measure of every part, maketh increase of the Body unto the edifying of itself in love" (Eph. 4:14-16).

✦ ✦ ✦

I NEVER knew until I became the father of children how much is involved in the words that occur in a well-known hymn,

> "No infant's changing pleasure
> Is like my wandering mind."

How children's minds jump from one thing to another! How hard it is for them to concentrate! And many of God's children are just the same. Very often when one is trying to open up some line of truth to believers, he is embarrassed by the questions that are asked showing that there is no concentration, no following up of the truth

already before them, and as a result people are
never truly established. It is in order to save us
from this thing that God has set in His Church
those who are responsible to instruct and build up
His saints, that they should not be like little children tossed to and fro, like leaves carried about
by the wind, or, using the figure the apostle has
in mind, like little sail-boats on the water, carried
hither and thither, blown from their course, and
tossed by every changing wind.

It is a blessed thing to see Christians who are
builded up by the Spirit of God in accordance
with the truth. But so many always seem to be
running after some new thing, never seeming to
have any discrimination. Let me give you an
absurd case. Years ago as I sat in my office in
Oakland there came in through the bookroom a
man whose very appearance betokened a heretic.
He was tall and gaunt, had long flowing hair coming down over his shoulders, and a long unkempt
beard. He came up to where I sat writing. I did
not like to be interrupted, for I felt that he was
going to waste my time with some religious odd-
ity. He said, "I gather, sir, from the books I have
seen in the window that you are a truth-seeker,
and I thought I would come in and have a chat
with you."

"You are mistaken," I said; "I am not a truth-
seeker at all."

"Oh, you are not; may I ask why you are not?"

"Why, because, sir, I have found Him who is the Way, the Truth and the Life, and therefore my seeking is at an end. Once I was a truth-seeker, but now I am a truth-finder, for I know Christ."

"Well, but are there not many things that you still need to know?"

"Oh, yes; there are a great many things that I need to know, but I have found the great Teacher, and I am not going around seeking truth any longer. He instructs me through His Word."

"Well, as for me, I am always seeking; I go anywhere and everywhere that I think I can learn more."

"Yes," I said, "I was reading of you in my Bible the other day."

"Of me?"

"Yes."

"What did it say about me?"

"It said, 'Ever learning, but never able to come to the knowledge of the truth.'"

"Why, that has no reference to me," he said.

"Pardon me, but you said that you are always seeking and if a man is always seeking he is never finding. But, you see, those of us who know Christ have found Him and have been found of Him."

Then he began to impart some of his weird gospel to me and said, "But you don't know who I am."

"No," I said; "beyond what is written here I do not know who you are."

"I am one of the 144,000 of whom you read in Revelation."

"What tribe, please?" I asked.

"Well, the Lord knows; I don't," he said.

"Then you will have to excuse me for not taking your word for it and really believing that you are one of the 144,000."

"But have you not heard that the first resurrection has already taken place?" he asked. "I am in my resurrection body."

"Is that it you have with you?"

"Why, yes; this is my resurrection body."

"Oh, I am dreadfully disappointed," I said. "I never thought it would look like that. I thought it was to be something beautiful."

Maybe I was a little discourteous to the poor old gentleman, but he was so indignant he turned and cursed me in the name of the Lord, and tramped out, knocking his shoes against the floor to shake off the dust as a witness against me. "Ever learning, and never able to come to the knowledge of the truth."

That is an extreme case, but what a lot of folks there are like him in some degree, just running from one thing to another and never getting anywhere. The apostle says, "Hold fast the form of sound words," and you get sound words in the Book of God and nowhere else.

"That we henceforth be no more children, tossed to and fro, and carried about with every wind of doctrine, by the sleight of men." That is, men who have selfish purposes to serve, and want to make disciples in order to profit from them. "And cunning craftiness, whereby they lie in wait to deceive." When men come to you with strange and new things, Christian, ask for a "Thus saith the Lord," ask them to give chapter and verse in God's blessed Book for the strange doctrines they bring you. If Christians would only do this, they would not be running after these modern religious fads. Here you have something that has stood the test of nineteen hundred years. It is God's own blessed Word, and you can depend upon it. You can live upon it and as you feed upon the precious truth here revealed you will grow in grace and in the knowledge of our Lord and Saviour, Jesus Christ.

But now, although we want to be very insistent upon a good confession we need to be just as insistent upon a godly life and upon the manifestation of the Spirit of Christ, and so in the next verse we read, "But speaking the truth in love, may grow up into Him in all things, which is the Head, even Christ." It is an important thing to stand for the fundamentals, but as we seek to bear witness to the great fundamental truths, let us never forget that the greatest fundamental of all is love. "Though I have the gift of prophecy, and understand all mysteries, and all knowledge; and though I have all faith, so that I could remove mountains, and have not love, I am nothing. And though I bestow all my goods to feed the poor, and though I give my body to be burned, and have not love, it profiteth me nothing" (1 Cor. 13:2, 3).

It is a very interesting fact that here in the original text there is only one Greek word for the three English words, "speaking the truth." In the original it is a present participle formed from the word "truth," and if we turn it into literal English we would have to render it in a rather awkward way. We would have to say "truthing." "But truthing in love." Perhaps a better rendering than "speaking the truth in love," and more suited to our ears, would be "manifesting the truth in love." In other words, it is not just the testimony of the lips, declaring that certain things are divine truth, but it is the life manifesting the truth. I have heard people say of certain ones, "Yes, yes; he seems to say things all right, but I do not see much evidence of divine love in his life." And then I have heard people sometimes bear witness of others in this way, "I believe in what Mr. So-and-So says because he lives it out from day to day."

A young man was asked the question, "What have you found to be the best translation of the New Testament?" Without a moment's hesita-

tion he answered, "My mother's." His friend
said, "Your mother's! I didn't know she was a
scholar. Did she translate the New Testament?"
"My mother was not a scholar, she could not read
a word of Greek, but she translated the New
Testament into her beautiful life, and that made
more of an impression on me than anything else
I have ever known." That is what you and I
are called upon to do, to manifest the truth in our
lives. The love of God has been shed abroad in
our hearts by the Holy Spirit which was given
unto us and now we are to be controlled by that
Holy Spirit. We are to manifest the love of God
in all our dealings with others. Even,

> "When truth compels us to contend,
> What love with all our strife should blend."

The Christian is never entitled to act in an un-
Christlike way, no matter what the provocation.
We are ever to be "truthing in love," and as we
thus live in the power of the truth of God and are
dominated by the love of Christ, we are growing
up into Him, daily becoming more like Himself.
Are people seeing more of Christ in you from
day to day?

I remember years ago a young preacher coming
to the city of Toronto, where I was born and
where I lived until I was ten years old, and though
I was only about eight years old at the time, I
recall being taken by my mother to hear this

preacher, for she insisted that I must go and
hear the gospel every Sunday night. She used to
say, "It is far more important that my children
hear the gospel than that they have sleep, or anything else. They must know Christ from child-
hood up." Of course in Canada our gospel meeting used to begin at 6:30 o'clock, and little folk
could attend and still be home and in bed in good
time. Before I was ten years old I got to be
quite a sermon taster, as the Scotch used to say.
I loved to come home and get on a chair and
take off the preachers, trying to give the intona-
tions of their deep Scotch voices or those from the
north of Ireland, for all the preachers I ever heard
in those days had the old country twang. I listened to this young Irish preacher, a fine, tall,
handsome young man. A little group came home
with us after the meeting to spend an hour or so
in singing around the old-fashioned cabinet organ.
Someone asked the question, "How did you like
the young preacher from Ireland?" One replied,
"It did me good to hear the old tongue again. It
was just grand." Another said, "I thought he
had a splendid delivery; you could hear him so
plainly." Another, "He seemed to me to be most
eloquent." Another, "How well he knew his
Bible. He opened up the truth in a beautiful
way." A lady sitting quietly was asked, "And
what did you think of him?" "Well, you know,"
she replied, "there was something about his be-

havior that appealed to me. He seemed the most like Jesus of any preacher I have ever listened to." How one might wish to have that kind of recognition—to be like Him. Some of us, as we try to preach His Word, are made very conscious of the fact that we are so unlike Him. There is so much about us that would never have been seen in Him. Never a night but one has to bow the knee before God and acknowledge it, but as we walk with Him, as we seek to "truth" in love, we grow up into Him, and so we become more like Him as the days go by.

It is a beautiful thing to grow old gracefully, to manifest more of Jesus from day to day. Our blessed Head is the One from whom we draw all our supplies for spiritual upbuilding, and we read, "From whom the whole Body fitly joined together and compacted by that which every joint supplieth, according to the effectual working in the measure of every part, maketh increase of the Body unto the edifying of itself in love." It is just the figure of the human body, and every part, every separate organ, every joint and sinew, every gland, working for the upbuilding of the whole. That is the ideal picture of the Christian Church and of Christian fellowship. Have you ever read "Hebich's Tub?" It tells the story of a quaint Dutch preacher over in the East Indies. Many years ago he was conducting religious services for a group of British army officers. He was characterized by a shrewd, keen humor and pressed the truth home in the most amazing illustrations. He happened to know that there were certain little dissensions among the group, and so on one occasion he took for his text, "That which every joint supplieth," and went on to read, "According to the effectual working in the measure of every part." He looked at his audience, and then with his eyes half-shut he said, "Did you effer see a tob? What iss it that makes a good tob? If you haff a good bottom to it, iss that a tob? No. If you haff a good side, iss that a tob? No. If you haff good hoops around it, iss that a good tob? No. But if you haff good boards for the bottom and fitly choined together, and then the good boards for the sides all fitly choined together, and then the good hoops and all of these things fitly choined together, you haff a tob. And it is the same with the Christian Church. You haff got to haff every believer in his place, and all fitly choined together by the power of the Holy Spirit. You may haff all choined together, but iff there iss a little pebble in between two of the staves, you do not haff a tob that will hold water. Iff the staves haff shrunk and drawn apart, it is useless, and iff I am a Christian and haff some selfishness in me, iff through selfishness or envy I do not haff real Christian fellowship, or iff little things come in, I am useless. Iff the Colonel's lady has some unkind feeling toward the Major's lady and they

come to church and join in prayer and in singing
hymns and listen to the sermon, yet they are not
fitly choined together, and you don't have real
Christian fellowship." How many little things
there are that come in to hinder and keep believers from functioning as they ought!

"Fitly joined together and compacted by that
which every joint supplieth." You have to contribute your share and I have to contribute mine,
all for the good of the whole. And then what?
"According to the effectual working in the measure of every part, maketh increase of the Body
unto the edifying of itself in love." May God
give every one of us a deeper sense of our individual responsibility to manifest the truth in
love for the blessing of all.

THE WALK OF THE NEW MAN

✓ ✓ ✓

"This I say therefore, and testify in the Lord, that ye henceforth walk not as other Gentiles walk, in the vanity of their mind, having the understanding darkened, being alienated from the life of God through the ignorance that is in them, because of the blindness of their heart; who being past feeling have given themselves over unto lasciviousness, to work all uncleanness with greediness. But ye have not so learned Christ; if so be that ye have heard Him, and have been taught by Him, as the truth is in Jesus: that ye put off concerning the former conversation the old man, which is corrupt according to the deceitful lusts; and be renewed in the spirit of your mind; and that ye put on the new man, which after God is created in righteousness and true holiness" (Eph. 4: 17-24).

✓ ✓ ✓

"THIS I say therefore"—we may well ask, "Wherefore?" In view of all that has come before us in the earlier part of this epistle, in view of the fact that we have been chosen in Christ before the foundation of the world that we should be holy and without blame before Him, in view of the fact that in love He has predestinated us unto the adoption of children by Christ Jesus unto Himself, in view of the fact that we have redemption through His blood, even the forgiveness of sins, according to the riches of His grace, in view of the fact that we have been made members of His Body, of His flesh, and of His bones, and are by the Spirit united to a risen Christ in glory—because of all these things, the apostle says, "I testify in the Lord, that ye henceforth walk not as other Gentiles walk." The Christian is called out from the world. His life is not to be as the lives of those about him. A very common saying is, "When you are in Rome, do as the Romans do," but that does not apply to the Christian. No matter where you find him, he is to walk as a heavenly man, as one whose interests are really in another scene, as a stranger and a pilgrim here. He is called upon to refrain from everything that would in any way tarnish his pilgrim character.

"Walk not as other Gentiles walk, in the vanity of their mind." The word translated "vanity" here does not mean what it does ordinarily. We usually think of it as meaning "pride." But the word here is not pride, the original word rather means something like a mirage, an illusion, that which is imagined but not actually true. Unsaved men have illusions of their own minds, they see mirages of all kinds and imagine them to be real, but they are not. They believe all sorts of theories, scholastic ideas, and such like, and would even bring this blessed Book to the bar of their theories instead of bringing their theories to the test of the Word of God. The Christian ought to be concerned about these things, and not walk in the delusions of the fleshly mind, for these poor Christless men, whatever their talents, whatever their culture, whatever their education, have the understanding darkened, have never been born of God, and are incapable of taking in divine things.

"The natural man understandeth not the things of God." I wish our Christian young people would realize that. I wish the Christian young men and women thronging our colleges (in many instances, unhappily, placed under the instruction of brilliant but unconverted professors, many of whom use their high office as an occasion to seek to undermine faith in the Word of God), could realize that the natural man, no matter what his intellectual qualifications, understands not the things of God; they are foolishness to him because they are spiritually discerned. Without a new life and a new nature there can be no real apprehension of divine things, and so the greatest of this world's sages is but as an ignoramus when it comes to the things of God, until he has been regenerated.

"Having the understanding darkened, being alienated from the life of God through the ignorance that is in them, because of the blindness of their heart." In other words, there is no divine life. Some say there is a divine spark in every man, but that is not true. "He that hath the Son hath life, but he that hath not the Son hath not life." Until Christ is received by faith, until peo-

ple have accepted Him as their own Saviour and
Lord, there is no life whatever except, of course,
this material, this natural life. "Being alienated
from the life of God through the ignorance that
is in them." They are wise as to the things of
this world, but utterly ignorant as to the things of
God. "Because of the blindness of their heart."
The word "blindness" is really "hardness," and
yet that does not give the thought sufficiently. It
means a heart that is under the influence of an
anesthetic. A person may be alive and quivering
with pain, but when he is put under the influence
of an anesthetic he is not awake to the true condition of things. Men and women have come
under the influence of the awful deadening power
of sin and their hearts are hardened, they are
blinded, and they do not understand the real state
of affairs, they do not understand their own condition, the condition of their country or of the
world around them. Sin has a terrible, harden-
ing, blinding, deadening, effect upon people. The
apostle describes the condition of the Gentile
world in his day. Any one who is at all familiar
with Greek and Roman literature, the literature
of the great poets of the ancients, particularly the
Comic poets, knows how very true is the description given here. How characteristic of society,
too, in the days in which we live. Is it not true
that the same fearful things that the ancients told
of without a blush are practised in the world to-

day in public and in secret? But Christians are called out from all this.

Notice the awfully graphic picture of the ancient world and the world today. "Who being past feeling have given themselves over unto lasciviousness, to work all uncleanness with greediness." "Being past feeling"—it might be translated, "Being beyond pain." Do you remember how pained you were the first time you committed some sin against which your conscience rebelled? The hour of temptation came, and you hesitated and said, "Shall I commit this sin or not?" Conscience was roused and you did not see how you could go on and indulge in that evil, unholy thing; but perhaps lured on by godless companions, who mocked at your conscientious scruples, you said, "Oh, I will try anything once," and you took the fatal step, you committed that sin and polluted your soul by it. But you remember the pain that came afterward, you remember as you walked home, or possibly it was in your own home, you could not bear the thought of facing those nearest and dearest to you. Perhaps you were not so much concerned about the fact that the eye of God was upon you as you ought to have been, but you were concerned about what others might think of you. The second time the temptation came, and again you plunged into the sin, more recklessly this time, and afterward the pain was less. And so, on and on and on, and now you continue in that sin, in that evil course, and there is scarcely ever the least evidence of an exercised conscience. We read of people whose conscience is seared as with a hot iron. Here you have the description of an unsaved man going contrary to every divine direction until he is beyond pain. That is what sin does for people. Oh, what a mercy when the Spirit of God comes in and awakens one to see something of the terribleness of sin in the sight of a holy God and leads him at last to Christ, and out of the depths of an anguished heart to cry, "What must I do to be saved? God be propitious to me, the sinner." There had been such crises in the lives of these Ephesians. Many of us have known what this means, and now these words of instruction come to us, as to them, regarding the walk that should characterize us.

We are not to be as we once were and as those still are who, having got beyond pain, have given themselves over to lasciviousness and all kinds of unholy thoughts resulting in unclean works. What a mercy that this is in the past for many of us. Am I speaking to anyone who is still living in these things? Does your heart sometimes cry out with a desire for purity, for holiness, for goodness? Do you sometimes say:

> "Tell me what to do to be pure
>   In the sight of all-seeing eyes.
> Tell me, is there no thorough cure,
>   No escape from the sins I despise?

Will the Saviour only pass by,
Only show me how faulty I've been?
Will He not attend to my cry?
May I not this moment be clean?"

Oh, yes; there is cleansing for you. "Come now, and let us reason together, saith the Lord; though your sins be as scarlet they shall be as white as snow; though they be red like crimson, they shall be as wool" (Isa. 1: 18). They tell me that two of our Chicago professors have gotten out a new Bible in which they have turned these two wonderful statements into questions, but I challenge any man who knows a word of Hebrew to look them up and see if they do not stand exactly as written in our Bible. It is the unbelief of the natural heart that would put a question-mark here, where God has made everything so clear. There is heart purity for the sinner, there is a possibility that the dark red stains of sin may all be washed away, for it is written, "The blood of Jesus Christ, God's Son, cleanseth us from all sin," and one thus cleansed should be characterized by an altogether different walk to that which is common to the unsaved.

The apostle goes on to say, "But ye have not so learned Christ; if so be that ye have heard Him, and have been taught by Him, as the truth is in Jesus." I want you to notice particularly the way he uses the divine titles. We know that Jesus is Christ and Christ is Jesus. We do not for one

moment consent to the wretched theory that a
good many hold today, the one that has been pop-
ularized by Mrs. Mary-Baker-Patterson-Glover-
Eddy in her false religion in which she tries to
draw a distinction between Jesus and Christ. According to that system, Jesus was simply a man,
the natural born son of Mary, but Christ was a
divine Spirit that came and took possession of
Jesus at His baptism in the Jordan. That is an
old gnostic heresy condemned by every right-
minded Christian. Jesus is the Christ. "Whosoever confesseth that Jesus is the Christ is born of
God." But although that is true, this is also true,
Jesus was His human name here on earth, He
never had that name until He came to earth.
Scripture says, "Thou shalt call His name Jesus;
for He shall save His people from their sins." But
He was Christ from all eternity. In the eighth
chapter of Proverbs, wisdom is personified, and
we read, "I was set up from everlasting, from the
beginning of His way, before His works of old."
The Hebrew term, "Set up," is the same word for
Messiah, or Anointed. "I was the Anointed, I was
Messiah from everlasting, I was the Anointed
from the past eternity." Then, when the Spirit
of God came upon Him after His baptism in the
Jordan, He was the Anointed, the Christ, in a
new sense. And when God raised Him from the
dead, we read He made that same Jesus to be
both Lord and Christ! He is the Anointed now
as the risen and glorified One.

And now Paul says, "Ye have not so learned Christ;" and he is thinking of Him as the risen One, Christ sitting at the right hand of God, and we learn of Him as we take time to behold Him. "But we all, with open face beholding as in a glass the glory of the Lord, are changed into the same image from glory to glory, even as by the Spirit of the Lord" (2 Cor. 3:18). "But ye have not so learned Christ; if so be that ye have heard Him, and have been taught by Him, as the truth is in Jesus." What does he mean by that? He means this, that when He trod this earth as the lowly Man, Jesus, in His life He was the manifestation of the truth. That is why He could say, "I am the Way, the Truth and the Life." Suppose I want to know the truth about man, what God's thought about man is, where do I find it? In Adam? Oh, no. In Adam I see a man who listened to his wife, after she listened to the devil, and did what she told him to do, a man without a backbone, a man utterly untrustworthy. Go down all through human history, and every other man is just a reproduction of that first man. But if I want the truth concerning man, I find that it is written, "There is one Mediator between God and men, the Man Christ Jesus," and so we see in Him as Man here on earth all that man should be for God. It is the full standard of humanity as God reveals it in His Word.

If I want to know the truth about God, where

do I find it? Do I go to the universities of this world? No; they do not know anything about God. They cannot tell me anything about Him. But where shall I go? To a lot of modernistic churches, with their unconverted preachers? They do not know anything more about God than unconverted college professors. Well, then, where shall I go? To Creation? Out in the woods? Out playing golf on Sunday? No, you will not find out about God there. You will get some evidences of His power and wisdom, but you will not find anything about His love and holiness there. Where do you learn about Him? In Christ. "He that hath seen Me hath seen the Father." The truth has been made known in Jesus.

Suppose I want to find out about sin, where will I go? To some of our modern, humanistic philosophies, to some of these teachers who talk about behaviorism and actually try to make men and women believe that every tendency within is perfectly lawful and perfectly right? No; not there. But where? In the cross of Jesus. There, as I behold Him, my blessed Saviour, taking the sinner's place, I see what sin deserved. The truth is in Jesus, and Christ in glory points me back to Jesus on earth and says, "If you want to know how you should walk as you go through this world, there is where you will find it." "Christ also suffered for us, leaving us an example, that ye should follow His steps" (1 Pet. 2: 21).

But how will I be able to walk like this? I have
an old nature, I once had a corrupt, sinful life,
how am I going to walk aright? Here is what
Jesus teaches. "That ye put off concerning the
former conversation the old man, which is corrupt
according to the deceitful lusts; and be renewed
in the spirit of your mind; and that ye put on
the new man, which after God is created in righteousness and true holiness." What do I mean
when I speak of the old man? Some people con-
found the old man with the old nature. You see,
the old man is more than the old nature. The old
man is the man of old, what you once were before
you were converted. Now you are through with
the man of old. If you are a Christian, you are
not to live like that man any longer, but you are
now to live in accordance with the truth of the
new man. And who is the new man? The new
man is the man of whom the Apostle Paul speaks
in 2 Corinthians 12: "I knew a man in Christ ...
of such an one will I glory." A man in Christ—
that is the man that I now am through infinite
grace. But I am through with the old man, the
man after the flesh. I have put him off, his tastes,
his appetites, all that he once delighted in, and I
am learning the truth as it is in Jesus.

The old man was corrupt according to the deceitful lusts, and in these we once walked in our
unconverted days. But now a great change has
taken place, we have been born again. That does

not mean we have attained perfection. The Apostle Paul said, "Not as though I had already attained, either were already perfect: but I follow after, if that I may apprehend that for which also I am apprehended of Christ Jesus. Brethren, I count not myself to have apprehended: but this one thing I do, forgetting those things which are behind, and reaching forth unto those things which are before, I press toward the mark for the prize of the high calling of God in Christ Jesus."

"And be renewed in the spirit of your mind." A better rendering is, "Being renewed in the spirit of your mind." In what sense am I being renewed in the spirit of my mind? How am I being renewed in my physical strength? As I am careful to eat those foods that are nourishing and that will help me to build a strong body. Then how am I renewed in the spirit of my mind? As I feed upon His Word, as I enjoy communion with Him, enjoy fellowship with His beloved people. In all these ways we are being renewed in the spirit of our minds. You never saw a strong Christian who was not a Bible-loving Christian. You never saw a strong Christian who was not one who delighted in communion with fellow-believers. Where you find people who cannot have anything to do with other Christians, who go about with the "I am holier than thou" attitude, you will never discern much real holiness in their lives.

"Being renewed in the spirit of your mind; and

putting on the new man, which after God is created in righteousness and true holiness." Righteousness is my behavior manward. I am to be
righteous in my dealings with my fellow-man. It
does not mean that I can be careful about my
devotion to Christ and careless in regard to my
life among others. A man got up in a meeting
one day and said, "I want to tell you that I am
standing in Christ on redemption ground." Another man arose and said, "I want to call that
man down. He says he is standing in Christ on
redemption ground. I do not believe a word of
it. He is standing in a pair of shoes he bought
from me months ago, and he has not paid for
them yet." Righteousness is right dealing between men. The person who professes to be a
Christian and is not careful about that which is
right, is a disgrace to the name of the Lord Jesus
Christ.

Holiness has to do with my attitude toward
God. It is of the heart, it is the inward life,
holiness of thought, a heart separated to God in
accordance with the truth of His holy Word. This
is practical Christianity, and this is how you and
I are called to manifest the new life, to manifest
the fact that we belong to a new creation.

Have I been setting the standard too high? I
have not been setting it at all. I have been giving
it to you from the Word of God.

Unsaved one, are you saying, "I should like to

reach this standard, but I do not see how I ever could"? You cannot. With all your trying you will never be able to reach it. Come to God as a poor, lost sinner, give up your trying, put your trust in the Lord Jesus Christ, and He will give you a new heart, a new nature, and will enable you to live to His glory.

GRIEVE NOT THE HOLY SPIRIT

✓ ✓ ✓

"Wherefore putting away lying, speak every man truth with his neighbor: for we are members one of another. Be ye angry, and sin not: let not the sun go down upon your wrath: neither give place to the devil. Let him that stole steal no more: but rather let him labor, working with his hands the thing which is good, that he may have to give to him that needeth. Let no corrupt communication proceed out of your mouth, but that which is good to the use of edifying that it may minister grace unto the hearers. And grieve not the Holy Spirit of God, whereby ye are sealed unto the day of redemption. Let all bitterness, and wrath, and anger, and clamor, and evil speaking, be put away from you, with all malice: and be ye kind one to another, tender-hearted, forgiving one another, even as God for Christ's sake hath forgiven you" (Eph. 4: 25-32).

✓ ✓ ✓

THE most important part of this entire section is verse 30, "And grieve not the Holy Spirit of God, whereby ye are sealed unto the day of redemption." The term, "grieve" means "to give pain." Give not pain to the Holy Spirit of God. How may we pain Him? By walking in disobedience to any of the admonitions that are given us in this particular section. We have here the behavior that should characterize a believer. We have seen something of our wonderful privileges, our great blessings in Christ in the heavenlies, and now we are considering that part of the epistle which stresses for us our practical responsibilities.

It is a poor thing to talk of living in the heavenlies if we are walking with the world. It is most inconsistent to glory in our privileges in Christ if we are behaving according to the flesh. And so here the apostle emphasizes the importance of true Christian living. He says, in verse 25, "Wherefore putting away lying, speak every man truth with his neighbor; for we are members one of another." We have seen how the exalted Christ in glory turns our hearts back to consider the blessed example set us by Jesus as He walked through this scene, that we may consider the truth as it is in Jesus. They came to Him on one occasion and said, "Whom makest Thou Thyself?" And He said (using the exact rendering), "Altogether what I say unto you." What a tremendous statement, nothing covered, nothing hidden, no sham, no pretence; He was exactly the same in the presence of God as He was before men. This indeed is truth in life, and you and I who have put our trust in Him are called to put away everything that is false.

The word translated "lying" is simply the Greek word that we have taken over into the English, *pseudo*—"that which is false." We are to put away everything that is merely pretence or sham, and speak every man truth with his neighbor. The Christian is called to be punctilious, to be honest even in little things, not to make bargains that he does not keep. If a business man, he is not to over-state the case when trying to sell something. In Proverbs we read, "It is naught, it is naught, saith the buyer: but when he is gone his way, then he boasteth" (Prov. 20:14). Even that is contrary to the Holy Spirit of God. The Christian is called on to be true in everything; true in his behavior, true in his speech.

Notice the motive given, "For we are members one of another." He is thinking especially here, of course, of our relation to fellow-believers, as though he would say, "Why should you attempt ever to deceive a fellow-believer? Why should you ever be false to another child of God? Why should you pretend to something that is not true when dealing with another Christian? Why should you be unfaithful to a member of the same Body to which you yourself belong?" Can you imagine members of our natural bodies being false to one another? What is for the good of one is for the good of all; and so in the Body of Christ, what is for the good of one member is for the good of all, and the Christian is called to see that he never defaults in any way in his dealings with a fellow-Christian.

Then we read in verse 26, "Be ye angry, and sin not: let not the sun go down upon your wrath: neither give place to the devil." This verse has perplexed many people. Some imagine that it is always wrong to be angry. There are circumstances under which it would be very wrong not to be angry. Our blessed Lord though absolutely perfect in His humanity was angry on more than one occasion. He saw the pretentious Pharisees going in and out of the temple of God with a great air of sanctity, and yet He knew some of them held mortgages on widows' homes, and when occasion arose they foreclosed on them and turned them out into the streets because they could not meet their obligations. Our Lord's indignation was aroused, His anger flamed up, and He said, "Woe unto you, scribes and Pharisees, hypocrites; for ye devour widows' houses, and for a pretence make long prayer: therefore ye shall receive the greater damnation" (Matt. 23:14). If my spirit would not be stirred to indignation by anything of the kind today, I am not the sort of Christian I ought to be. If I were to see a great brute of a fellow abusing a little child and were to pass by with that sweet simpering Christian Science smile that says, "Oh, well; everything is lovely; God is good and good is God; all is God and God is all, and there is nothing wrong in the world," and would not be stirred to anger, I would be a cad and not a Christian. There is an anger that is righteous. We read that our Lord Jesus on one occasion "looked round about on them with anger, being grieved for the hardness of their hearts." How, then, am I to be angry and sin not? A Puritan has put it this way, "I am determined so to be angry as not to sin, therefore to be angry at nothing but sin."

You see the moment self comes in, my anger is sinful. You do me a wrong and I flare with anger. That is sin. But you blaspheme the name of my Saviour and if I am not stirred to anger, that is sin. If I am wholly reconciled as I should be, it will arouse my indignation when I hear His name blasphemed, or see the truth dragged in the dust. But so far as I am concerned, I am to suffer all things, I am to endure all things. Men may count me as the offscouring of the earth, they may do the worst they can against me, but if I become angry, I sin, for self is the object there.

Who is there then that is sinless? No one. That is why He says, "Let not the sun go down upon your wrath." If you are stirred to sinful anger, if you flare up, see then that you do not retire to your bed at night before you confess your sin. If you have given vent to indignation before another, see that you confess it to him. Many people have said to me, "I have such a bad temper. I have tried so hard to overcome it, but I get angry and say things that I regret afterwards, and I make up my mind never to do it again, but I am sure to fail." I usually ask this question, "Do you make it a practice, when you have given utterance to angry exclamation, to go to the person before whom you have sinned and confess it?" Sometimes I get this answer, "No, I never cherish anything; I flare up, and then it is all over." Yes, but the memory is not all over. The other person remembers it. If every time you sin through anger you would go immediately to the one sinned against, and confess and ask forgiveness, you would soon get tired of going so often and you would put a check upon yourself. It would not be so easy to fly off the handle. But as long as you can flare up and pay no attention to it, or, while you may confess it to God you do not do so to your brother, you will find the habit growing on you.

This expression, "Be ye angry, and sin not," is a direct quotation from the Septuagint translation of Psalm 4:14. Our English version reads, "Stand in awe, and sin not: commune with your own heart upon your bed, and be still." The Hebrew word translated, "stand in awe" is a word that means, "tremble," and our translators rendered it, "Stand in awe"—tremble at the presence of God. But that is not necessarily all that it means. The Septuagint made it read, "Be ye angry, and sin not." These words were probably recorded at the time that David was fleeing from Absalom, his own son, and his heart was stirred as he thought of the unfilial character of his son's behavior. That son for whom he had so often prayed was bringing dishonor upon the name of the Lord, and it moved his heart to indignation. But he said, "I am not going to sleep tonight until all that indignation is quieted down —'Stand in awe, and sin not: commune with your own heart upon your bed, and be still.'" Just get quietly into the presence of God and then you will be able to look at things from a right standpoint, and as you think of your own failures, of the many, many times that God in grace has had to forgive you, it will make you very lenient as you think of the failures of others, and instead of getting up on the judgment-seat and judging another believer, it will lead you to self-judgment and that will bring blessing, whereas the other is only harmful to your own spiritual life.

"Let not the sun go down upon your wrath: neither give place to the devil." Why? Because anger cherished becomes malice, and Satan works through a malicious spirit. He seeks to get control of Christians and have them act in malice toward fellow-believers. All this grieves the Holy Spirit of God. These are searching things, and we have to take them each for himself. "The Word of God is quick, and powerful, and sharper than any two-edged sword, piercing even to the dividing asunder of soul and spirit, and of the joints and marrow, and is a discerner of the thoughts and intents of the heart" (Heb. 4: 12). Let us not avoid it but face it honestly.

"Let him that stole steal no more: but rather let him labor, working with his hands the thing which is good, that he may have to give to him that needeth." There is many a person who steals who would not like to be called a thief. We have names for stealing that sound much better, for instance, "pilfering," and "purloining." They mean the same thing but do not sound quite as bad as "stealing." But the Spirit of God covers them all in this, "Let him that stole steal no more." Let him that appropriated that to which he had no right, steal no more. The Christian is to be intrinsically honest. You know, it is easy to become slack along these lines. It is easy, if you are working in an office, for instance, to say to yourself, "Oh, well; they don't pay me anything like what I am worth, and therefore there are certain little things about the office I can claim." I knew one young man who had a habit of stealing lead pencils until he had accumulated a gross of them, and then his conscience smote him, and the day came when he had to go back to the boss with the lead pencils and say, "I am a Christian and I am returning these pencils to you." Christians are called upon to be faithful in very small things, things that others may not pay any attention to at all. What a pity that sometimes Christians cannot be trusted. The child of God ought to be one who can be trusted anywhere, one who will be faithful in another man's things just as much as in his own things.

But it is not enough that we refrain from thievery. The Law says, "Thou shalt not steal," but grace comes in and how much higher is the standard set under grace than that under Law! It is not only, "Let him that stole steal no more," but he adds, "But rather let him labor, working with his hands the thing which is good, that he may have to give to him that needeth." I could live up to the righteousness that is in the Law if I refrained from taking what is another's, but I cannot live up to the holiness of grace except as I share with others what God in His kindness gives to me. What a wonderful standard is that of Christianity.

And then in verse 29 we have the care of the tongue. The Psalmist says, "Set a watch, O Lord, before my mouth, keep the door of my lips." And James says, "If any man offend not in word, the same is a perfect man, and able also to bridle the whole body" (James 3:2). I have met some "perfect" people. I knew they were perfect because they told me so; but when I was with them a while and listened to their speech, heard their careless, worldly chatter, noticed how critical of other people they were, heard the unkind, cutting remarks they could make concerning other people, I knew their perfection was all a delusion.

"If we say we have no sin, we deceive ourselves and the truth is not in us." Here the apostle says, "Let no corrupt communication proceed out of your mouth." Corrupt communication comes from the old nature which is corrupt. You see, the new nature produces holy communication; the old, the corrupt nature, produces corrupt communication. "Let no corrupt communication proceed out of your mouth, but that which is good to the use of edifying, that it may minister grace unto the hearers." "Oh," says somebody, "this is where my trouble is. My tongue is always getting into difficulty. I make up my mind never to say anything unkind, and the next instant my tongue seems to be set on a pivot." Very well, when you find that you just must talk and you cannot stop, say, "Now, Lord, this tongue of mine wants to get going; help me to say something good." And then quote some Scripture and speak of the grace of the Lord Jesus Christ, tell that which is good for the building up of your hearers, and you won't go away with regrets and at the close of the day have to get down on your knees and say, "O Lord, forgive me for my careless chatter and un-Christianlike words today." We are not cut out to be dumb, some of us like to talk, but we are to talk about good things, we are to let Christ be the burden of our speech, to present Him to others.

I have known men with whom it was a delight

to spend a little time because I never went from their company without learning more of the Lord Jesus. I am thinking of a friend of mine in whose company I have never been for ten minutes but what he would say to me, "You know, I was thinking of such and such a scripture, and while I was meditating the Spirit gave me such and such a thought." How different it is with others at times. How different it has been many, many times with this tongue of mine. What sorrows it has brought upon me, speaking unadvisedly with the lips. "Let no corrupt communication proceed out of your mouth, but that which is good to the use of edifying (that is, for the building up of those to whom you speak) that it may minister grace unto the hearers."

And now we come to the crucial text—"And grieve not—pain not—the Holy Spirit of God, whereby ye are sealed unto the day of redemption." As we have already seen, the Spirit of God dwells in each believer, a divine Person, a blessed, heavenly Guest, and He is listening to everything you say and is taking note of everything you do. All that is said, all that is done contrary to the holiness of Christ and to the righteousness of God, grieves that blessed indwelling Holy Spirit. Have you ever known what it was to have some one in the house who did not approve of anything you were doing? Perhaps they did not say anything, but you had the sense that

they did not like things. That is the way it is
with the Spirit of God if a believer is not walking
in accordance with the truth.

Do we read, "Grieve not the Holy Spirit of God,
lest you should grieve Him away?" No, you are
not going to grieve Him away. Jesus said, "I
shall send you another Comforter, that He may
abide with you forever." When He comes to indwell a believer, He never leaves. David, in the
Old Testament dispensation, said, "Take not Thy
Holy Spirit from me," but in the glorious dispensation of grace, that prayer is not becoming to
our lips, for when He comes to indwell us, He
never leaves us until we are presented faultless in
the presence of the Lord Jesus Christ. But the
point is just this, He does not leave, He dwells
within, but is grieved all the time that we are
walking in disobedience to the Word. That is
why many of us are never very happy; that is
why we do not enjoy communion with God, that
is why we are not singing songs of victory. You
see, as long as the Holy Spirit dwells in me un-
grieved He is free to take of the things of Christ
and show them unto me, and that fills my heart
with gladness. But the moment I begin to grieve
Him He stops doing the work He delighted to do,
He is not free to open these things to me. He has
to occupy me with my own failure and sin until
I confess it.

Then, I have the joy of knowing that I am

sealed—how long? "Unto the day of redemption."
What does he mean by that? Is not the day of
redemption the day Christ died on Calvary's
cross? That was when Jesus died to redeem my
soul. But there is the coming day of the redemption of the body when the blessed Lord will return
again to transform these bodies of our humilia-
tion and make them like unto His own glorious
body. It is the redemption referred to in Romans
8:22, 23: "For we know that the whole creation
groaneth and travaileth in pain together until
now. And not only they, but ourselves also, which
have the first-fruits of the Spirit, even we ourselves groan within ourselves, waiting for the
adoption, to wit, the redemption of our body."
We are sealed unto the redemption of our bodies.
When we get that, the old nature will be gone, we
will not have to be on our guard any more against
grieving the Holy Spirit. It is here and now in
this body that we need to watch against this
thing.

He concludes this section by saying, "Let all
bitterness, and wrath, and anger, and clamor, and
evil speaking, be put away from you, with all
malice." I wish that as Christians we would let
the Word of God have its way with us! Is there
any bitterness in your heart against any one on
earth? Do you say, "But you don't know how I
have been tested, how I have been tried, insulted,
offended?" If you had not been offended there

would be no reason for the bitterness at all, but he says, "Let all bitterness, and wrath, and anger, and clamor, and evil speaking, be put away from you, with all—a-l-l—malice." Now, you see, if you do not live up to that, you are not living a real Christian life. This is Christianity in the power of the Holy Ghost. And we are not merely told to put these things away, there must be the positive side.

"Be ye kind one to another, tender-hearted, forgiving one another, even as God for Christ's sake hath forgiven you." To what extent must I forgive? "I have forgiven over and over and over again, and I cannot go on forgiving forever," you say. Wait a minute. What does the apostle say about the extent to which we are to forgive? "Even as God for Christ's sake hath forgiven you." Can you ever get beyond that? Has any one ever wronged you as much as you wronged God? But if you have trusted the Saviour, God in Christ has forgiven you all your trespasses. Now this is the standard for Christians, we are to forgive one another even as God in Christ has forgiven us.

CLEAN CHRISTIANS

✓ ✓ ✓

"Be ye therefore followers of God, as dear children; and walk in love, as Christ also hath loved us, and hath given Himself for us an offering and a sacrifice to God for a sweet-smelling savor. But fornication and all uncleanness, or covetousness, let it not be once named among you, as becometh saints; neither filthiness, nor foolish talking, nor jesting, which are not convenient; but rather giving of thanks. For this ye know, that no whoremonger, nor unclean person, nor covetous man, who is an idolater, hath any inheritance in the kingdom of Christ and of God. Let no man deceive you with vain words: for because of these things cometh the wrath of God upon the children of disobedience. Be not ye therefore partakers with them" (Eph. 5: 1-7).

✓ ✓ ✓

THE city in which the church was found to which this letter was addressed, abounded with iniquity of the vilest kind, and it was therefore of great importance that the early Christians should be warned of the danger of following in the ways of those still in their sins, and it is just as necessary today. The human heart is unchanged and with all our veneer of civilization unmentionable vilenesses are practised throughout the length and breadth of our land, enough to cause every Christian heart to shudder and make one feel the importance of living very close to the Lord Jesus Christ that we may be kept from these evil things.

Notice upon what the apostle bases the call to clean living. "Be ye therefore followers of God, as dear children." "Therefore," that is, of course, because of what he has told us in the previous verses. He has told us that God for Christ's sake has forgiven us; which means that God thought enough of us to send His only begotten Son into the world that we might live through Him, that God was as in Christ reconciling the world unto Himself, not imputing men's trespasses unto them; but those trespasses were imputed to Him, the Holy One, when He took our place and bore our shame, endured the judgment due to our sins —because of this, let us walk now in such a way as to manifest the gratitude of our hearts for so great salvation. "Be ye therefore followers of God, as dear children."

The word rendered, "followers," really means "imitators." "Be ye therefore imitators of God." In what sense are we to imitate God? One thinks of a passage in the Old Testament where God said to His people, "Ye shall put out of the camp of Israel every leper"—every one who hath any kind of a vile, infectious disease; not only for the safety of those who were not yet infected, but the singular thing about it was that back in the Law the reason given is this, "Because ye shall be holy, for I the Lord thy God am holy." And as in the legal dispensation all physical uncleanness was looked upon as a thing accursed and not fit for the holy presence of God, so today all uncleanness of the flesh and spirit must be put away if we would walk in fellowship with the Holy One. To imitate Him in holiness of life, to imitate Him in purity of thought, to imitate Him in cleanness of speech as His dear children, children in whom He can delight—this is what we are called upon to do.

You parents know how there are times when your own children, much as you love them, cause you sorrow and grief if they walk in disobedience, if they fall into anything that dishonors the family name, anything that grieves your heart, and so it is with God's children. The least sin indulged in by His children grieves the Holy Spirit. If we would be His dear children, in the sense of children in whom He can delight, we must walk before Him as imitators of God and "walk in love, as Christ also hath loved us, and given Himself for us an offering and a sacrifice to God for a sweetsmelling savor." The reference here, of course, is to the burnt offering. In the burnt offering spoken of in the first chapter of Leviticus we have the offerer coming to God with a sacrifice, not merely because of any sin committed, but because his heart is filled with thanksgiving and he wants to present something to God as an expression of his loving adoration. And so there is one aspect of the work of our Lord Jesus Christ on the cross that rises far above the mere meeting of our need; it has in view the glorifying of God in the scene where He had been so terribly dishonored.

The Lord Jesus said to His disciples on the last night on which He was betrayed as they sat with Him at the table, "That the world may know that I love the Father, and as the Father hath given Me commandment even so I do. Arise, let us go hence." And He went out to die. Why did He endure that death upon the cross? His first object was the glory of the Father. God had been terribly dishonored by the first man and all that had come after him, but here at last was a Man who walked this scene in absolute holiness. He said, "I seek not Mine own will, but the will of the Father which hath sent Me" (John 5:30), and to do the will of God He went to that cross. He went there to settle the sin-question for us, but above everything else it was to show that at least one Man had been found to whom the glory of God meant more than anything else, to whom the will of God meant more than any personal desires that He Himself might have had. And so in Gethsemane's garden we hear Him saying, "Nevertheless not as I will, but as Thou wilt." This is the great Burnt Offering. He offered

Himself without spot *to God* a sacrifice of sweet-smelling savor. But we are not left out. He offered Himself *for us,* a sacrifice of sweet-smelling savor to God for us. And since we have thus been redeemed, what manner of persons ought we to be in all holy conversation and godliness?

It is always with a shock that the sensitive soul turns to the next verse, and is brought up against terms that speak of the vilest corruption of which the human heart is capable. This is given that we may realize that all these things must be judged if we would now walk with Him who has redeemed us to God. And so we read, "But fornication, and all uncleanness (impurity), or covetousness, let it not be once named among you, as becometh saints." The word rendered "covetousness" does not refer here to greed for money. It is, rather, sensual greed. It is that vile, disgusting greed for sensual gratification, the vilest thing of which the human heart is capable. Is it possible that saints of God need to be warned against these things? Yes; because in every believer there is the same corrupt nature that there is in the man or woman of the world. It is true that the saint has received a divine nature and the Holy Spirit of God has come to dwell in him, but, nevertheless, he must always watch against the least activity of that old nature lest he fall into sin through not judging its first motions toward that which is evil.

"Fornication, and all uncleanness" (or sensual greed). These things are in the very air around us. Modern literature is full of them, and the worst of it is that people glory in their vileness. But some say, "Well, our modern writers at least are very frank; they show up sin as it really is." Yes, frank enough in the way they speak of it, disgustingly so, and yet they seem to throw a halo about it as though these unclean things are so natural to human beings that no one need be ashamed of them. And the world is fast getting to the place our Lord Jesus Christ predicted it would just before His second coming. He said, "As it was in the days of Noah, so shall it be also in the days of the Son of Man," and, "As it was in the days of Sodom and Gomorrah so shall it be at the coming of the Son of Man." The days of Noah were days of great corruption and violence. The days of Sodom and Gomorrah were days of unmentionable vileness, and we are living in very similar times. All of our boasted civilization has not changed the tendency of the human heart one iota, and the child of God is to guard against every evil tendency. The first approach to it is always in the mind, and so He warns against impure thoughts. We are not to indulge in thoughts that are impure. We are to guard against lust of every description. Can you think of any greed more dreadful, more vile, more disgusting than that which would lead one to plot the ruin of an innocent young girl's life? It would break the heart of parents who have tried to bring up a precious daughter in the right way, if one came in and sought to turn her away from the path of goodness and purity. Can you think of anything more dreadful than an attempt to break up a happy home by coming between husband and wife, turning one or the other aside from the path of rectitude and right? And yet these things abound everywhere. This is the greed about which the apostle warns us. The pathetic thing is that people look with such indifference upon these things.

Notice what we read in verse 4, "Neither filthiness, nor foolish talking, nor jesting, which are not convenient: but rather giving of thanks." Every word here needs careful consideration. The apostle is not warning us against that bright, happy conversation which leads people sometimes to exchange agreeable thoughts and give vent to lively natural humor. He is not calling us to be long-faced, unhappy people who do not dare to tell anything that provokes an innocent laugh. In fact, I am rather afraid of these people who are so holy that they cannot laugh. A good, hearty laugh is a healthy thing. God meant man to laugh. That is the one thing that distinguishes him from all the other creatures. Until scientists can find a monkey who can laugh, they will never find the missing link! God rejoices over His people and laughs in scorn when men think to thwart His will. The apostle is thinking here about something against which every Christian needs to be on guard. He has warned against these sins, and now he says, "Let it not be once named among you, as becometh saints." It is even defiling to talk about it, even to pass on the news that other people have fallen into those things. If as servants of God we have to do with these things, we find it necessary to get into the presence of God in prayer, for they leave their effect upon the heart and mind.

"Neither filthiness," that is, indecency—do not talk of indecent things. "Nor foolish talking," which really means buffoonery, making a jest, talking like a fool about unclean things. You know people who do that, people who jest of unclean things, people who think it bright, smart, to use words of double meaning, words that bring the blush to the cheek of a beautiful Christian young woman, or even trouble a right-thinking Christian young man. It literally means, "a fool's talk," and the man who talks this way demonstrates that he is a fool. The word "jesting" is really "ribaldry," and is another word that implies in a deeper sense making jest of things that should never be talked about. Christians should be clean, Christians should be like their blessed Lord, clean in thought, in word, and in deed.

In place of these things, what should occupy

the Christian tongue—"Rather giving of thanks."
There is a beautiful play in the Greek language
that does not come out very clearly in the English.
The word translated "jest" and the term "giving
of thanks" begin exactly the same. The Greek
for the one is *eutrapalia,* the Greek for the other
is *eucharistia.* You can see how the apostle was
just balancing the one word against the other.
Not *eutrapalia* but *eucharistia;* that is, not ribaldry but thanksgiving, not vile talk but praising the Lord, not filthy conversation but that
which brings glory to the Lord Jesus Christ. On
one occasion I was attending a conference of
Christians and a number of us were guests at the
home of a very devoted believer. As we gathered
between meetings one day in the beautiful draw-
ing-room, a lady suddenly said, "Well, now, we
will go out and help our hostess get the dinner
ready." Possibly fifteen men were left together.
A man who had just come in remarked, "Since
the ladies have gone out, there is a story I got
hold of today I would like to tell you." Before
any one else had a chance to speak, a friend of
mine said, "Just a minute, brother; there are no
ladies here, but the Holy Ghost is here and is
more sensitive than the most fastidious lady. Is
your story fit for Him?" The man was big
enough to say, "Thank you, Mr. B——, I accept
the reproof. I will never tell such a story again."
Remember, the Holy Spirit of God is grieved if

believers stoop to any of the things mentioned here.

And now the apostle warns us that if any reject such instruction as we have here and live in uncleanness, they simply give evidence that they are not Christians at all. They are children of the devil wearing the livery of Christ. "This ye know, that no whoremonger, nor unclean person, nor covetous man, who is an idolator, hath any inheritance in the kingdom of Christ and of God." Why does he couple idolators with these other things? Because this kind of a beast worships only himself. What does he care if he breaks other people's hearts? What does he care if he wrecks young lives, breaks up homes? He must satisfy his own base cravings. He worships one god; that god is himself. It is absurd for a man like that to profess to be a Christian.

When I think of the stories that those of us who are ministers of Christ have to hear—of the hundreds of broken-hearted young women who have come to me and told the awful story of their betrayal, of the breaking down little by little of their higher ideals and the ruin that has come, I feel the greatest punishment that their betrayers could bear would be to have to listen forever to such stories and know that they were responsible for them. When I have had fathers and mothers come and sit weeping as they have talked of one who was once the joy of their home, the

love of their hearts, and tell how she had been
lured away into sin, and their hearts were broken
and they could no longer find the joy in their
child they once did, I have said, "If these betrayers of innocent girls would only have to sit in the
confessional and listen to stories of this kind year
after year, it would be a fitting punishment." And
people like that profess to be Christians! "But,"
you say, "they are sometimes in the church."
More shame to them, coming under the cover of
the church and pretending to be what they are
not in order to go on in their vile, sinful way!
Christians ought to be clean, Christians ought to
be pure, because Christians are children of the
Holy One, the Holy God.

"Be not ye therefore partakers with them."
While one may pray for them, yet there is to be
no fellowship with them, no condoning of their
vile deeds. They should be made to feel that they
are unclean lepers until their sins are confessed
and judged, and they have given evidence of being
delivered from them. God give us Christians to
walk in love, that love which would ever preserve
us from working any harm to any one else, that
love which would lead us ever to seek the good of
others, and never in any sense their hurt, even
"As Christ also hath loved us, and hath given
Himself for us an offering and a sacrifice to God
for a sweetsmelling savor."

You may say, "But what if some have fallen

into just such things; is there no hope?" No hope until the sin is judged, no hope until it is confessed, no hope until with earnest desire to be completely delivered from it they turn to Him who is the Holy and the True, and cast themselves in penitence and faith upon His atoning work. Then, trusting Him, they will find that He gives them a new heart and a new life, and makes them lovers of purity and goodness.

THE FRUIT OF THE LIGHT

✓ ✓ ✓

"For ye were sometimes darkness, but now are ye light in the Lord: walk as children of light: for the fruit of the Spirit is in all goodness and righteousness and truth; proving what is acceptable unto the Lord. And have no fellowship with the unfruitful works of darkness, but rather reprove them. For it is a shame even to speak of those things which are done of them in secret. But all things that are reproved are made manifest by the light: for whatsoever doth make manifest is light. Wherefore He saith, Awake thou that sleepest, and arise from the dead, and Christ shall give thee light" (Eph. 5: 8-14).

✓ ✓ ✓

THIS section immediately follows the exhortation to personal purity. We have seen that those who have been redeemed to God by the precious blood of His beloved Son are called to be clean in thought, in word, and in deed. And that message was addressed to a people who were living in an impure and vicious environment such as we know very little of in our day. We may shrink with horror from conditions prevailing about us, but nineteen centuries of gospel testimony have made men very much ashamed of many things which they once did shamelessly. In the days when the apostle wrote, things were practised openly which now go on only in private. If Paul could write to Christians in his day exhorting to that purity which we have seen should characterize them, how much more should you and I today, who confess the name of our Lord Jesus Christ, flee everything that has to do with uncleanness or immorality of any kind.

The clear light of God's holiness is to be our standard. "Ye were sometimes darkness, but now are ye light in the Lord: walk as children of light." Do you notice that he does not say, "Ye were sometimes in the dark," but, "Ye were darkness." Darkness is ignorance of God, and we were once, in our unconverted days, in ignorance of God and therefore said to be "darkness." We did not have the Light of life. Every natural man is in that condition. Job asked the question, "Can a man by searching find out God?" and the answer is in the negative, for all philosophizing or reasoning about divine things ends in confusion because men in their natural state are darkness.

"The natural man understandeth not the things of God because they are foolishness unto him." They are spiritually discerned. We were once in that condition, and when in that darkened state, we walked in darkness, and practised things of which we are now ashamed. But having become children of the light, being born of God, and made light in the Lord, we are to walk as becometh children of the light. You remember what is said of our Lord in the first chapter of John: "In Him was life; and the life was the light of men." Did you ever stop to meditate upon those words? In our Lord Jesus Christ divine life was fully manifested, for He was "that eternal life which was with the Father and was manifested" unto men. Now John says, "The Life was the light of men," or, as he puts it in another place, "That was the true Light which coming into the world casts light on every man" (*Lit. Trans.*). Even if He uttered not a word, His pure and holy life, ever in subjection to the Father, was in itself the condemnation of all sinful men. "The Life was the light." You and I are children of the light, and we possess that same life which our Lord Jesus Christ is. He is the eternal life and He has communicated eternal life to us. That life is now to be manifested as light.

A lady said to me some time ago, mentioning a certain servant of Christ, "Did you ever know Mr. So and So?" "Oh, yes," I said, "I knew him well." "Well," she said, "you know, we had him in our home for a month and his very presence there seemed to change everything for us. Why, there was such godliness about it, piety without long-facedness, holiness without morbidity. Our children simply loved him, and yet there was such

intense godliness that soon the little things that
they used to do and say carelessly, dropped away.
They did not like to say in his presence what
they would when he was not there, they did not
like to do when he was looking the things that
ordinarily they would do with utter indifference.
The effect of his presence in our home was simply
wonderful and yet he never reproved anybody by
word of mouth for anything they did or said, but
he manifested the life, and the life was the light."
We have known the other kind also. I have had
the privilege of having in our home all sorts and
conditions of preachers and Christians, and we
have had some of them that our children fairly
loved and were always glad to welcome because
of their Christlikeness and devotedness, and I
have had others who have made the boys gnash
their teeth when they came up the walk. I can
recall now one good man who seemed to think it
was his business to run the house when he was
there. If a child was a little slow to obey or a
bit pert, as children sometimes are, instead of
leaving the discipline to his parents, he would
exclaim, "That child ought to be spanked!" You
can imagine the effect on the children. You can
imagine how they loved to hear a man like that
preach, how they would want to see him as a
visitor in our home! It is not the person who
goes around constantly finding fault with other
people who accomplishes the best results. He

only stirs up the flesh, arouses the enmity of the natural heart to things that are pure and good. But the man who lives Christ, the woman who manifests life eternal in the home, among friends, in the Church, these are the people whose testimonies really count for God. "The Life is the light."

You remember how the Apostle Peter emphasizes that when he addresses wives who have unconverted husbands. He says to them in First Peter 3: 1-4, "Likewise, ye wives, be in subjection to your own husbands: that, if any obey not the Word, they also may without the Word be won by the conversation of the wives; while they behold your chaste conversation coupled with fear. Whose adorning let it not be that outward adorning of plaiting the hair, and of wearing of gold, or of putting on of apparel; but let it be the hidden man of the heart, in that which is not corruptible, even the ornament of a meek and quiet spirit, which is in the sight of God of great price." I wonder if our sisters these days have ever noticed this passage. Here is a woman who has been brought to Christ, and her husband is still in paganism, or in Judaism, as the case may be, and she is deeply interested in his conversion. What is to be her attitude? Constantly nagging and talking and reproving? Oh, no; but her behavior is to be so sweet and Christlike and gracious that as he looks upon her he will say,

"Well, my wife has something now she did not have before. She used to be so ready to speak up and answer back, and now she is so sweet and gracious. I wonder what it is that she now posesses that is so contrary to what characterized her by nature."

"If any obey not the Word...they may without the Word be won." In the first clause it is the Word of God that is meant. In the second instance it means, without speech, without nagging. It might be paraphrased thus: "Likewise, ye wives, be in subjection to your own husbands, that if any obey not the Word of God they also may without nagging be won by the good behavior of the wives." And the same principle applies to every one of us. It is not merely something for our sisters to consider, but those of us who are men are called upon to manifest the truth we profess, not by constant finding fault with people, not by criticizing and trying to set everybody and everything right by word of mouth but by manifesting the life of Christ, the purity of Christ, the love of Christ in our lives. This is to walk as children of the light.

"For the fruit of the light" (in our Authorized Version it is, "The fruit of the Spirit," but in the Revised Version it reads "light") is "in all goodness and righteousness and truth." Here then are the graces that should characterize those who are children of the light. It is not enough to profess to believe on the Lord Jesus Christ, to submit to Christian baptism, to take the communion at the Lord's Table, to be members of some Christian assembly or congregation, but we are required to manifest the fruit of the light in our lives. Where there is life there is fruit. Where there is only a dead profession you will not find fruit, but where people are truly born of God there will be fruit. "By their fruits ye shall know them." "Even a child is known by his doings, whether his work be pure, and whether it be right" (Prov. 20: 11). Children who have taken the name of Christ upon them are responsible to produce the fruit of the light, and if they act in a wilful or wayward manner they should immediately go to the blessed Lord and confess it. Their lives should be different from the lives of other children who have not yet accepted Christ. Whether young or old we are to manifest the fruit of the light.

What is this fruit of the light? "For the fruit of the light is in all goodness." The word literally means "benevolence," "kindly consideration for other people." If you are really born of God, you possess a new and divine nature, you will follow the footsteps of the Lord Jesus Christ, and of Him we read, "The Son of Man came not to be ministered unto, but to minister, and to give His life a ransom for many." "He laid down His life for us: and we ought to lay down our lives

for the brethren" (1 John 3:16). Have we ever
thought of that? "We *ought.*" That is a word
that speaks of duty. "To lay down our lives for
the brethren." That is the opposite of selfishness.
The world says, "Number one first." But we are
called to be considerate of others first. Some one
has well said that heavenly grammar is different
from worldly grammar. In ordinary grammar
you take the persons: first person, I; second per-
son, you; third person, he or she. But in Christianity it is: first person, he or she; second per-
son, you; and third person, I. In Christianity
I come in last, I am not to put myself first. When
I am thinking of comforts, I am to think of others
first. But how different it is with many of us.
We are content if we do a little from time to time
for somebody else in wretched circumstances,
whereas we are called to live for Christ daily and
to manifest the fruit of the light continually,
which is in all goodness.

And then in the second place, "The fruit of the
light is in all righteousness." Now righteousness
is simply doing right. What an amazing exemplification of the unrighteousness of the human
heart we have seen within the last few years!
Trusted officials in banks, big business men who
were looked up to and thought to be absolutely re-
liable, have in many instances proven to be unrighteous men handling other people's money dis-
honestly, unfaithful to their trust. What a lot of

suicides have followed our bank failures. How fast our penitentiaries are filling up with men who a short while ago were looked upon as perfectly dependable, and yet our modern theologians are still dreaming that human nature is not corrupt, and that "every fall is a fall upward."

A friend of mine riding on the street-car handed the conductor a gospel tract. When the conductor's busy time was over, he walked down the aisle of the car to my friend and said, "You handed me this?"

"Yes."

"Why did you give it to me? I have no interest in these things."

"But that is a gospel message."

"I do not need the gospel. It is for sinners, but I do not believe in sin, and I do not believe that man is a fallen creature."

"That is peculiar," my friend said; "why have you that machine at the door of the car?"

"Oh, that is to count the money."

"But why do they need it for men like you in whom there is no sin?"

Theologians can talk about an improved race and a sinless race and deny the fall of man, but business men know differently. The rule today is, "Do not trust anyone until he proves that he is not a rogue." Christian, be careful about attempting to witness for Christ by word of mouth if you are not manifesting the fruit of the light in

your ways. Be sure that behind your testimony
there is a righteous life.

The third thing, "The fruit of the light is in
truth." Righteousness, as we have seen, has to
do with your actions towards others. Truth has
to do with your own inward sincerity. "Thou
desirest truth in the inward part: and in the hidden part Thou shalt make me to know wisdom"
(Ps. 51: 6). Years ago when I was a young Salvation Army officer, on one occasion our Colonel
came to address us. Quite a group had come in
from all over the State for an officers' council.
I have never forgotten through all these years
the faithful words of the Colonel. He said, "Now,
remember, comrades—men will forgive you if you
are not educated, they will forgive you if your
culture is not up to the highest standards, if you
are not eloquent, if you cannot sing charmingly,
but they will never forgive you if they find out
that you are not sincere, that you are pretending
to be what you are not." When Christ dwells in
us, we will be real, we will be genuine in our dealings with God and with men.

"Proving what is acceptable unto the Lord."
In other words, "Testing what is acceptable unto
the Lord." Not so ready to say, "I think this is
all right; I do not see any harm in that," and
run off to do as we will, but considering first, "I
am a Christian and am indwelt by the Holy Spirit
of God. Is this thing what Christ would have?

Will this bring glory to my blessed Lord? If I say this, if I do that, if I go here, will I really be honoring my Saviour?" In that way we "test what is acceptable unto the Lord."

And then on the other hand, "Have no fellowship with the unfruitful works of darkness, but rather reprove them." As we have already seen, we are really proved by the lives we live. The Christian cannot expect to be kept from contamination of sin and evil if he goes on in fellowship with iniquity; you might as well expect a child to play about in the filth and slime of the streets and not be contaminated, as to expect a Christian to go on in fellowship with wickedness and not be affected by it.

This is one of the scriptures together with many others that have exercised my own conscience through the years and kept me from a great many associations into which I would otherwise naturally have gone. When years ago such questions arose as to whether I would affiliate myself with certain secret societies and lodges of various kinds, the question at once arose, Are they composed of born again people? If I do join them, will it mean fellowship with the unfruitful works of darkness? Will I be walking in the path laid down for me by Christ? For the Lord has said, "Come out from among them, and be ye separate, and touch not the unclean thing; and I will receive you, and will be a Father unto you, and ye shall be My sons and daughters" (2 Cor. 6: 17, 18). That scripture kept me out of many things. But I have gained immensely, for the time I would have spent in some of those associations I have been permitted to spend with the people of God or over the Word of God. Do not be afraid that you will ever lose by obedience to the Book.

The strength of the Christian is in his separation from the world and his devotion to Christ.

Verses 13 and 14 are intimately linked together. "But all things that are reproved are made manifest by the light: for whatsoever doth make manifest is light." He has said, "Have no fellowship with the unfruitful works of darkness, but rather reprove them." That he does not mean mere fault-finding is evident from the words, "All things that are reproved are made manifest by the light." That is what is needed. Just turn on the light and it will show up everything that is contrary to it. In other words, you live the pure, holy, Christlike, godly, devoted life, and that in itself will be reproof enough of the iniquity abounding upon every hand. "All things that are reproved are made manifest by the light: for whatsoever doth make manifest is light." John tells us in his epistle, "God is light, and in Him is no darkness at all." Light is the very nature of God, and the moment one comes into the presence of God he is made manifest as a sinner, but he sees there in the presence of God the precious blood upon the mercy-seat which tells of the sin question settled and sin put away, and thus he enjoys peace with God through our Lord Jesus Christ. And so he walks in the light unafraid because he is in Christ.

The danger is that one may accept all this in the head only. "Wherefore he said, Awake thou that sleepest, and arise from the dead, and Christ shall shine upon thee" (R. V.). It is not possible to find any one Old Testament scripture that contains these words in their exactness. They are rather a free rendering of Isaiah 60: 1. There the Spirit of the Lord speaking through the prophet says, "Arise, shine; for thy light is come, and the glory of the Lord is risen upon thee." The apostle takes that word "arise" to mean, "wake up out of your sleep," as when you go into the boy's room in the morning and say, "Tom, it is time to arise!" Many who profess to be Christians are like people sleeping in a cemetery, sleeping among the dead with their heads pillowed upon the gravestones! You who are children of the light (this is not a message for the unsaved but for those who are saved and have gone to sleep): "Awake, and arise from the dead, and Christ shall give thee light." "Come out from among them and be ye separate." Show by your life that you are different from the unsaved worldlings about you.

Do you want blessing? Do you want a sense of the light of His face shining upon your life? Do not tolerate any hidden wrong; put it right, make confession. Maybe it is a letter you ought to write, maybe an acknowledgment you ought to make, maybe some money you ought to return. Do you say, "I can't afford it"? But it is not yours, you know. Put things right and then trust God for the rest. Righteousness first, and other things will follow. "Awake, thou that sleepest, and arise from the dead, and Christ shall shine upon thee."

THE FILLING WITH THE HOLY SPIRIT

✔ ✔ ✔

"Se then that ye walk circumspectly, not as fools, but as wise, redeeming the time, because the days are evil. Wherefore be ye not unwise, but understanding what the will of the Lord is. And be not drunk with wine, wherein is excess; but be filled with the Spirit; speaking to yourselves in psalms and hymns and spiritual songs, singing and making melody in your heart to the Lord; giving thanks always for all things unto God and the Father in the name of our Lord Jesus Christ; submitting yourselves one to another in the fear of God" (Eph. 5: 15-21).

✔ ✔ ✔

WE are now occupied with the walk of the believer. "See then that ye walk circumspectly, not as fools, but as wise." This is the seventh time that the word "walk" occurs in this epistle. I think it will be profitable to go back and notice the occurrences.

In chapter 2: 2 we have the past tense. If we were to include that, it would mean the eighth time, "Wherein in time past ye *walked* according to the course of this world." This was how we used to live when we belonged to the world. But we who are saved are delivered from that and so we read in verse 10 of the same chapter, "For

we are His workmanship, created in Christ Jesus
unto good works, which God hath before ordained
that we should *walk* in them." We are not saved
by good works, but we are to walk in good works
after we are saved. In chapter 4:1 we read, "I
therefore, the prisoner of the Lord, beseech you
that ye *walk* worthy of the vocation wherewith
ye are called." Having been called with a heavenly calling, we are now to walk, to behave ourselves, as a heavenly people. Following that, in
verse 17 of the same chapter we read, "This I
say therefore, and testify in the Lord, that ye
henceforth *walk* not as other Gentiles walk, in the
vanity of their mind." In our unconverted days
we walked in the pride and folly of the human
mind at variance with God, but as believers we
are not to do this any more, but we are to walk
in lowliness and in obedience to the Word of God.
Then in chapter 5:2 we are told to, *"Walk* in
love, as Christ also hath loved us, and hath given
Himself for us an offering and a sacrifice to God
for a sweetsmelling savor." In verse 8 we read,
"Ye were sometimes darkness, but now are ye
light in the Lord: *walk* as children of light." And
now in verse 15 the apostle says, "See then that
ye *walk* circumspectly, not as fools, but as wise."

Our English word, "circumspectly" means
"looking all around," like one who is walking in
a very dangerous place. There are pitfalls on
this side, quagmires on that side, traps and snares

all about. And so this person as he walks is constantly observing where he should next place his feet. That is a circumspect walk, a walk looking all around. Christian, your path leads you through a world of sin, a world of folly, a world where you are exposed to all kinds of temptations and unholy influences. Snares and traps abound for your unwary feet. Therefore, walk circumspectly, be careful where you put down your feet, be careful as to the company you keep, be careful as to your behavior in any company, so that there be that which will bring glory to the Lord Jesus Christ. Walk not as fools, not as simple ones, not as those who are still darkness, but walk as wise men—made wise by the wisdom of God.

"Redeeming the time, because the days are evil." The apostle uses this expression in one of his other letters, and in each instance it literally means, "Buying up the opportunities." Just as people go out bargain hunting and say, "There, if I buy that today, I can get it at a good price, much better than if I have to let it go until another time. It is worth my while to buy these bargains up at this rate." Let the Christian be just as eager, just as earnest, to obtain opportunities to witness for Christ, to serve the blessed Lord, and to be a means of blessing to others with whom he comes in contact. Buying up the opportunities, seeking to use them to the glory of our Lord Jesus, realizing that the days are evil and the time for serving Christ is slipping fast away, and that opportunities once lost will never be found again. Therefore, the importance of buying them up while we have the chance.

"Wherefore, be ye not unwise, but understanding what the will of the Lord is." And mark it, the only way that you and I can be delivered from our own natural foolishness, is by being divinely enlightened. We do not understand what the will of the Lord is excepting as we give ourselves to the careful, thoughtful study of His Word. Years ago I used frequently to stop in the midst of a discourse and ask everyone in my audience who had read the Bible through once to raise his hand. The last time I did that I was so ashamed that I made up my mind never to do it again. I had an audience of five hundred people, all of whom professed to be Christians, and when I put that question to them, only two raised their hands, and I was ashamed to have the devil see it. I was so thankful that there were not a lot of sinners there to see it. They would certainly say, "Those Christians do not value their Bible very much." I am reminded of something that occurred just recently in this city. There was an open religious forum down town. Clarence Darrow was there to represent the Atheists, another to represent Protestantism, another Roman Catholicism, and another, Judaism. The Catholic got up and told why he was a Catholic, and the Protestant got up and told why he was a Protestant, the Jew why he was a Jew, and then Clarence Darrow, the Atheist, got up to speak, and he said, "Gentlemen, I have been very much interested in one thing. I notice neither Protestant, Catholic, nor Jew ever referred to the Bible. Evidently they no longer value that so-called Holy Book as they used to do." And then he went on to declare that he was an Atheist because he had no use for the Book that they never even mentioned. What a pitiable thing that professed Christians should attempt to tell why they were Catholic or Protestant and never once refer to the Bible! Oh, that you and I might be genuine Bible Christians!

A friend of mine used to be designated as a walking Bible, and I thought, What a splendid description! If anybody ever came and said, "Mr. So-and-So, what do you think about such and such a thing?" he would say, "Let us see what God says about it," and out would come his Bible. "Why," the man would say, "I didn't know it was answered in the Book that way." I never knew this friend to say, "I think," but always, "God's Word says so and so." If you and I would be wise with the wisdom that cometh from above, we need to search the Scriptures. I like that little chorus:

> "In my heart, in my heart,
>   Send a great revival;
> Teach me how to watch and pray,
>   And to read my Bible."

The pitiable thing is that the great majority of Christians, I dare say, are so busy with other things that they have very little time for their Bibles. Although engaged exclusively in Christian service now for forty-five years, I do not dare come into the pulpit, I do not dare undertake my day's work without first going to the Word of God to gather fresh manna from day to day. If sometimes I am so hurried in the morning because of being out very late the night before and over-sleeping a little, or an urgent call comes and I rush out thoughtlessly without going to the Book, I find myself saying, "What is the matter with me today? I feel so dried up and half-starved spiritually. I am in no condition to try to minister to other people." And then the answer comes, "Why, you didn't have your spiritual breakfast this morning. You went off without a bit from God's Word," and I have to say, "Lord, forgive me for thinking that anything is more important than time spent with Thyself."

If you are not in the habit of reading your Bible methodically, prayerfully, let me beg of you, let me plead with you, go into the presence of God and confess to Him the sin of thus neglecting His Holy Word. He says, "Search the Scriptures," and if you disobey a command, it is sin. If you have been disobedient go to Him and confess it, and say, "Lord, henceforth teach me to say with Thy servant, 'Neither have I gone back from the commandment of His lips; I have esteemed the words of His mouth more than my necessary food' " (Job 23:12). Give God the first place in your life, give His Word the place it ought to have and then indeed you will understand what the will of the Lord is.

And now the apostle continues, "And be not drunk with wine, wherein is excess; but be filled with the Spirit." You will notice he puts two things in opposition, the one to the other—drunkenness with wine and the filling of the Holy Spirit. Why does he contrast these two things, these two conditions? You see, the man who has been over-imbibing, the man who is drunk with wine, is controlled by a spirit foreign to himself. Men, when they are under the influence of the spirit of alcohol, do and say things that they never would do in their normal condition. They make fools of themselves, they descend to all kinds of ribaldry and nonsense, and people say, excusing them, "Oh, well; you mustn't hold it against him; he is drunk, he is not himself." The apostle says that that condition should never be true of a Christian, but on the other hand the Christian should be dominated and controlled by a Spirit other than himself. He should be controlled by the Holy Spirit of God, and in the power of the Holy Spirit one is enabled to say and to do what he could not say and do in his merely natural condition. And so the filling of the Holy Spirit ought

to be the normal experience of every believer—
"Be not drunk with wine, wherein is excess; but
be filled with the Spirit." The word here is not
really in the past tense but in the present—"Be
habitually filled with the Holy Spirit."

What is the filling with the Holy Spirit? I
think the thought that a great many people have
is that it is some strange, ecstatic, emotional experience that comes to them at a given moment
and then later passes away and has to be repeated
again. But that is not it. This is the normal experience of the Christian life: "They were all
filled with the Holy Ghost, and they spake the
Word of God with boldness" (Acts 4:31). They
were dominated, they were controlled by the
blessed Holy Spirit of God, and this does not
necessarily result in any special emotional break-
down, but rather preserves one in the path of
orderliness and common sense. In the second
Epistle to Timothy we read, "God hath not given
us the spirit of fear; but of power, and of love,
and of a sound mind." I have been in some
places where people talk a great deal about the
fulness of the Spirit and where I have seen things
that I never would have thought possible a few
years ago outside of an insane asylum, people
rolling upon the floor and raving like maniacs,
and yet calling that the fulness of the Spirit. That
is not the spirit of a sound mind. The man who
is filled with the Holy Spirit does not go off into

some wild, fanatical state, but walks thoughtfully and carefully with God, and his testimony has power with men.

Turn to the Epistle to the Colossians, chapter 3 : 16, "Let the word of Christ dwell in you richly in all wisdom; teaching and admonishing one another in psalms and hymns and spiritual songs, singing with grace in your hearts to the Lord." Notice the effect there of the Word of Christ dwelling richly in the soul. Then turn back to Ephesians and read these verses again. Do you observe that you get the exactly the same results in Colossians when the Word of Christ dwells in you richly that you get in Ephesians when you are filled with the Spirit? What then is the inference? There is an old rule in mathematics that "things equal to the same thing are equal to one another." If to be filled with the Word is equal in result to being filled with the Spirit, then it should be clear that the Word-filled Christian is the Spirit-filled Christian. As the Word of Christ dwells in us richly, controls all our ways, as we walk in obedience to the Word, the Spirit of God fills, dominates, and controls us to the glory of the Lord Jesus Christ. Therefore, if you would be filled with the Spirit and you know of anything in your life which is contrary to the Word of God, if you are tolerating anything in your private life which is contrary to the Word of God, if there is anything in your outward associations, in your behavior before the world that is contrary to His Word, go into His presence, confess your sins, sins of omission, sins of commission, deal with it all before Him, and when everything has been uncovered and faced in His presence, dare to believe that He means what He says when He declares, "If we confess our sins, He is faithful and just to forgive us our sins, and to cleanse us from all unrighteousness" (1 John 1:9). And now, seek grace from Him to walk in obedience to His truth, cry out from the depths of your heart as the Psalmist did, "Order my steps in Thy Word" (Ps. 119:133), and as you walk on in obedience to the Word of God, you will be filled with the Spirit.

Do not get the idea that you must have some remarkable outward demonstration, some amazing sign that the Spirit of God has actually taken possession, but remember that He dwells in every believer, and as you give Him room, He cleanses out of you everything that hinders. As you let Him take full possession you are filled with the Spirit. What will be the evidence of it? One will be fulness of joy. The Holy Spirit is a Spirit of gladness, the Spirit of joy. Now do not misunderstand me, there is a difference between holy joy and mere natural merriment. Take the life of our blessed Lord Jesus Christ. Even though He was the Man of Sorrows and acquainted with grief, as we read the records in the four Gospels

we cannot help but be impressed with the fact
that we are not reading the life of a sad Man but
of a glad Man. "At that time Jesus rejoiced in
spirit and said, Father, I thank Thee." That
is characteristic of the blessed Lord. In spite of
all the grief and sorrow that He bore He was
joyful. But having said that, let me remind you
that in these records you do not see depicted what
the world calls a jolly man. His was no mere
worldly jollity, no mere worldly merriment, but
a deep-rooted gladness that was based upon un-
broken communion with the Father, and that is
the joy that you and I should possess. The
one who is filled with the Spirit will be a glad,
joyous believer.

"Speaking to yourselves in psalms and hymns
and spiritual songs, singing and making melody
in your heart to the Lord." It might be translated, "Speaking to one another." The world con-
siders that a man who talks to himself is a bit
queer, but that is not always the case. It is well
sometimes for us to sit down and talk to ourselves about things in our lives. What the apostle
is saying here is really, "Speaking to one another,
to the entire company." How? "In psalms and
hymns and spiritual songs." As we meet with
one another, greeting each other in a glad, happy
way, the praises of the Lord bubble up in our
souls. Psalms were the vehicle of expression in
the congregation of God in olden times. The book

of Psalms was the hymn-book of the congregation
of the Lord in ancient times, and there are wonderful expressions there that suit every mood of
the human heart. While we do not rise to the
height of the Christian's privilege in the book of
Psalms yet we can find something to express
every state and condition of our souls as we come
into the presence of God. A hymn is an ascrip-
tion of praise addressed directly to the Deity.

"Holy, Holy, Holy! Lord God Almighty!
Early in the morning our songs shall rise to Thee."

How the Christian heart naturally goes out to
God in hymns of worship and adoration. No
more worldly songs for the Christian. The day
is gone, or should be, when he can sing the worldly songs. I always think a Christian has dropped
from the high level on which he belongs when I
hear him singing such songs, because he has
something better, he has spiritual songs, songs
that tell of the love of Christ, of what grace hath
wrought, that tell of redemption by the precious
blood of Jesus. Who would sing the old songs
when we have learned the new?

"We will sing of the Shepherd that died,
    That died for the sake of the flock,
His love to the utmost was tried,
    But firmly endured as a rock;
We will sing of such subjects alone,
    None others our tongues shall employ,
Till fully His love becomes known,
    In yonder bright regions of joy."

One reason that the spirituality of the Church is at such a low ebb today is because people are so careless about matters of this kind, so ready to drop down from the high and holy state that should characterize those that are filled with the Spirit of God.

"Singing and making melody in your heart to the Lord." We cannot all make melody on an instrument. Some of us would never be able to produce any melody if dependent upon an instrument, but every believer's heart is like a harp, and as the Spirit of God breathes over the heartstrings, real melody goes up to the ear of God.

And now, the Spirit-filled believer will be a thankful believer. "Giving thanks always for all things unto God and the Father in the name of our Lord Jesus Christ." "Oh, but," you say, "there are some things I cannot give thanks for, there are some things so hard, so difficult to bear, there are some things that lacerate my very soul." Wait a moment. Have you ever undergone a serious physical operation as a result of which you have been delivered from something that was just wearing out your very life? When you had to undergo it, it seemed very hard, but as you look back upon it, can you not give thanks for the surgeon's knife, can you not give thanks for the very sufferings you had to endure because of the blessed after-result? Very well, Christian, some day.

> "When we stand with Christ in glory,
> Looking o'er life's finished story,"

we shall see as we cannot now just why all the
hard things were permitted, and how God our
Father was seeking to set us free from hindrances
and from encumbrances, by pruning the branches
from which He wished to get fruit for Himself.
In that day we will thank Him for all the sorrow
as well as for all the joy. In faith let us do it
now.

Nothing can come to me but what His love
allows. "All things work together for good," and
so a Spirit-filled believer will be loyal and sub-
missive, not the kind who tosses his head and
says, "I am not going to have anybody dominate
me; I will do what I think and what I like."
That is the old walk of our unconverted days,
that is the old nature, not the new.

"Submitting yourselves one to another in the
fear of *Christ*," as the better version reads. He
was God manifested in Christ. The Spirit-filled
believer, then, is characterized by these three
things, joyfulness, thankfulness, lowliness. May
God give to each one of us to be filled with the
Spirit.

THE CHRISTIAN FAMILY

✦ ✦ ✦

"Wives, submit yourselves unto your own husbands, as unto the Lord. For the husband is the head of the wife, even as Christ is the Head of the Church: and he is the saviour of the body. Therefore as the Church is subject unto Christ, so let the wives be to their own husbands in everything. Husbands, love your wives, even as Christ also loved the Church, and gave Himself for it; that He might sanctify and cleanse it with the washing of water by the Word; that He might present it to Himself a glorious Church, not having spot, or wrinkle, or any such thing; but that it should be holy and without blemish. So ought men to love their wives as their own bodies. He that loveth his wife loveth himself. For no man ever yet hated his own flesh; but nourisheth and cherisheth it, even as the Lord the Church: for we are members of His Body, of His flesh, and of His bones. For this cause shall a man leave his father and mother, and shall be joined unto his wife, and they two shall be one flesh. This is a great mystery: but I speak concerning Christ and the Church. Nevertheless let every-one of you in particular so love his wife even as himself; and the wife see that she reverence her husband" (Eph. 5: 22-33).

✦ ✦ ✦

YOU will notice how intimately verse 22 is linked with verse 21: "Submitting yourselves one to another in the fear of God." This is a principle of Christian living which applies to believers in every relationship of life, and now that the apostle turns to consider the Christian family he shows that it applies there. Did you ever stop to think what a wonderful institution the Christian family is? In reading a letter from a missionary in a heathen land I was struck by a paragraph which read something like this:

"How we wish that some of our Christian people could come and settle among us, even if not to engage in missionary work. There are different ways by which one might make his living among this semi-civilized people. For instance, we might have a Christian dentist and his wife, or a Christian worker in leather, a shoemaker, harness-maker, and his wife and family. It would mean a great deal to us to have a harmonious family here, for we can conceive of nothing that could so commend Christianity to our people as just to see a Christian family functioning according to the New Testament. It would be so utterly different from anything our people have ever known. A Christian husband loving and honoring his wife, a Christian wife living in sweet and beautiful subjection and loyalty in her home, Christian children who really delight in obedience to their parents, parents who love their children and seek to bring them up in the nurture and admonition of the Lord." This is something that is unknown in many heathen lands. It is Christianity, it is the knowledge of Christ, that produces the Christian home, and how jealous we should be of this blessed and delightful institution.

It is a very remarkable thing that in this letter the writer leads us up to the highest heights of divine revelation, to that which thrills our souls, as he speaks of our being predestinated according to the riches of grace to a place that angels have never known, accepted in the Beloved, blessed with all spiritual blessings in heavenly places in Christ. Then in the closing portion he seems to descend to what we might consider very commonplace. He applies this wonderful body of truth to the behavior of a Christian family. It is a poor thing to talk high truth while living on a low level in the home. I am afraid there are those who can repeat very glibly the statements of the first half of the Epistle to the Ephesians and delight in the wondrous privileges that belong to the people of God, who fail wretchedly when it comes to exemplifying the truth in the last half of this epistle in the daily life; and yet that is simply the truth of the first chapters made practical.

"Submitting yourselves one to another in the fear of God." And then immediately you have the exemplification of that in the relationship of the husband to the wife. Look at the verse: "Wives, submit yourselves unto your own husbands, as unto the Lord." If you happen to have the Revised Version, you will see that the words, "submit yourselves" are in italics, and correctly so. That means that they are not found in the best manuscripts. Let us read it exactly as it is in the Greek: "Submitting yourselves one to another in the fear of God, wives unto your own husbands, husbands loving your wives." Do you see? He is not calling upon the wife to take the place of a slave—she often takes that place in pagan lands—but he is calling for mutual loyalty, mutual respect, mutual submission. Pass over the intervening words to verse 25, "Husbands, love your wives, even as Christ also loved the Church, and gave Himself for it." That is how the husbands submit themselves unto the wives, so it is a mutual thing. That which makes the Christian home what it ought to be is this mutual loyalty, the one to the other, the wife to the husband, the husband to the wife. This is a marvelous thing when you think of it.

Here is a beautiful young woman. She has had her own way to a large extent, she has made her own way through the world, perhaps, or she may have come from a home where she has been carefully nurtured and cared for. By-and-by she meets a man, no blood relation of hers whatever, yet somehow or another her heart goes out to him, and she says, "For his sake I would be willing to go to the ends of the world, face all kinds of experience, keep house for him, care for his and my children, take the place of loving submission." It is a man whom a little while ago she did not know. Or, here is a man; he has made his own way, gone on into that period of his life when the world dubs him a bachelor. He has made his own money and could say what he would do with it and with his time. But he meets a woman to whom his heart goes out and he says, "For her dear sake I am willing to work and toil and labor, and if it means to impoverish myself to care for her, I will gladly do it." That is the Christian ideal, and when the Spirit of God dwells in each heart, what a beautiful picture it becomes of the mutual relation of Christ and the Church! And you see, it is exactly the same thing that takes place in the spiritual world.

Here was one going on in his own way utterly independent of God, but he is brought face to face with Christ, and his heart says, "For His sake I resign my own way; I give Him control of my life; I trust myself to Him; I am willing for His name's sake to go and do whatever He would have me do." Christ on His part laid down His life to purchase the one He loves, and now delights to lavish blessings upon this one whom He has made His own. We shall never know the fulness of this until we get to heaven. He has designed that every Christian home should exemplify this very thing.

How we ought to challenge our hearts as to how far our homes harmonize with this blessed picture that the apostle brings before us here! Let us examine each verse somewhat carefully. "Submitting yourselves one·to another in the fear of God, wives unto your own husbands, as unto God." Remember, it is only of a Christian family that directions like these could be given. Here is marriage not only in the flesh but in the Lord. What a sad thing for the Christian ever to contemplate marriage apart from subjection to the Lord. "Be ye not unequally yoked together with unbelievers," is a word that applies here as well as to many another relationship of life. "For the husband is the head of the wife, even as Christ is the Head of the Church: and the saviour of the body."

Our blessed Lord Jesus Christ as the Head of the Church undertakes now to provide for the Church, care for it, minister to it in all its necessities. So the Christian husband is the one, not to lord it over others in a harsh, arbitrary, masterful way, but to exemplify the gracious care of the Lord Jesus Christ as the saviour of the body. And so the Christian husband charges himself with the support of the wife and the family. He is ready to toil and labor that they may be kept in a measure of comfort and ease, and because of this, as the Church is subject to Christ so should the wife be to her own husband.

On the part of the husband we read in verse 25, "Husbands, love your wives, even as Christ

also loved the Church and gave Himself for it."
A dear young fellow who had but lately taken to
his heart and home a beautiful bride came to me
in distress one day and said, "Brother Ironside,
I want your help. I am in an awful state. I am
drifting into idolatry."

"What is the trouble?" I asked.

"Well, I am afraid that I am putting my wife
on too high a plane, I am afraid I love her too
much, and I am displeasing the Lord."

"Are you indeed?" I asked. "Do you love her
more than Christ loved the Church?"

"I don't think I do."

"Well, that is the limit, for we read, 'Husbands, love your wives, even as Christ also loved
the Church, and gave Himself for it.' "

You cannot get beyond that. That is a self-
denying love, a love that makes one willing even
to lay down his life for another.

You remember that striking story about the
wife of one of Cyrus' generals who was charged
with treachery against the king. She was called
before him and after trial condemned to die. Her
husband, who did not realize what had taken
place, was apprised of it and came hurrying in.
When he heard the sentence condemning his wife
to death, he threw himself prostrate before the
king and said, "O Sire, take my life instead of
hers. Let me die in her place!" Cyrus was so
touched that he said, "Love like that must not be

spoiled by death," and he gave them back to each other and let the wife go free. As they walked happily away the husband said, "Did you notice how kindly the king looked upon us when he gave you a free pardon?" "I had no eyes for the king," she said; "I saw only the man who was willing to die for me." That is the picture that you have here. That should characterize the Christian husband—willing to lay himself out to give of his best, even of life itself, for the blessing of his dear ones.

"Husbands, love your wives even as Christ also loved the Church, and gave Himself for it; that He might sanctify and cleanse it with the washing of water by the Word." It is as though the apostle can scarcely speak on this subject but that it brings before him the One who has won his own heart, and he must tell us more about Him. This blessed Husband, this glorious Head of the Church, this ideal for every Christian husband, gave up His own precious life for the Bride of His heart, the Church, that He might sanctify and cleanse it with the washing of water by the Word. Some imagine that this is a reference to baptism, a kind of sacramental washing, but I take it rather that the words explain themselves. He has found us in our sins, in our uncleanness, unfit for association with Him, the Holy One, but He applied the water of the Word of His truth to us and we were sanctified by the truth and made fit to enter into this communion with Him, the Holy and True One. If my hand becomes defiled, I wash it in water and the defilement disappears. So when my conscience, my heart, my life were all defiled, the blessed Lord by the Holy Spirit applied the truth of His Word to me and I was regenerated by the washing of water, and thus made clean in His sight, and so fitted for union and communion with Him. By-and-by the full regeneration will be seen in glory when He shall present His Bride to Himself, a glorious Church, not having spot occasioned by sin, or wrinkle occasioned by age.

In Revelation 21 : 2 we read, "And I John saw the holy city, the New Jerusalem, coming down from God out of heaven, prepared as a bride adorned for her husband." This is the glorious picture of the Church as it will be throughout all the ages to come—"without spot or wrinkle or any such thing." There are some of my brethren who in their hyper-dispensational teaching can read this chapter and deny that the Church is the Bride of the Lamb. They tell us that Israel is the Bride. But the apostle says the Bridegroom is the blessed Lord; the Church, His redeemed spouse, and the two are linked together for eternity. He then applies it to us again, "So ought men to love their wives as their own bodies. He that loveth his wife loveth himself." The two have become one now, and therefore, the man who would treat his wife unkindly is as one who would destroy or injure, or cause grief to his own flesh, and so we may put it contrariwise. We have heard of wives who are so vixenish in their tempers that they cause even good and devoted husbands unspeakable anguish. Both are one flesh, and need to learn that, "No man ever yet hated his own flesh; but nourisheth and cherisheth it, even as the Lord the Church." For so intimate is our union with Him that, "We are members of His Body, of His flesh, and of His bones."

If some insist that the Church is the Body but not the Bride, the very argument that the apostle uses contradicts them. The Church is both the Body and the Bride even as a man's wife is both his body and his bride. And so it was written in the book of Genesis: "For this cause (because of this union) shall a man leave his father and his mother, and shall cleave unto his wife: and they twain shall be one flesh." What a marvelous thing it is when two are thus brought together through divine grace, the Lord having first united their hearts to Himself and then to each other, and so they set up a Christian home.

Is your home such as the apostle is here depicting, where husband and wife walk together in mutual love and subjection, and where Christ is ever honored? If not, it would be well to inquire why it is not. Perhaps you would find that the true root of the trouble is in the neglect of the family altar. May I turn you to another passage of Scripture? 1 Peter 3:1, "Likewise, ye wives, be in subjection to your own husbands: that, if any obey not the Word, they also may without the Word be won by the conversation of the wives." Here you have a case where there is no spiritual unity in the family—where the husband is not a Christian and the wife is. Look at verse 7, "Likewise, ye husbands, dwell with them according to knowledge, giving honor unto the wife, as unto the weaker vessel, and as being heirs together of the grace of life; that your prayers be not hindered." Here you have the Christian relationship—"that your prayers be not hindered." Notice those words. When a Christian home is the way it ought to be, prayer like fragrant incense will rise unhindered to God the Father from that family altar. But where the home is not as it should be, where husband and wife are not subject to one another, where there is not that delightful relationship, then prayer immediately is hindered. There—may I say?—you get the thermometer that shows what conditions are in the home. What a blessing when husband and wife can happily kneel together and bring their varied problems to the Lord, or together lift their hearts to Him when things are going well. But when there is reserve on the part of either one or the other, you may know there is a storm in the offing, or something has already taken place hindering their fellowship and communion.

If in your home the family altar has not been
set up, see to it that not another day goes by
until husband and wife read the Word together
and kneel together in the presence of God, com-
mending one another and the children to the Lord.
You will find it will make a great difference, and
day by day anything that would hinder prayer
can be judged there at the family altar.

In closing this section, the apostle says, "This
is a great mystery." He has spoken again and
again of mysteries in this epistle. In chap. 1: 9
he says, "Having made known unto us the mystery of His will." In chapter 3: 3-5 he says, "By
revelation He made known unto me the mystery,
which in other ages was not made known unto
the sons of men, as it is now revealed unto His
holy apostles and prophets by the Spirit." And
now he says, "This is a great mystery." What
is a great mystery? Why, this question of the
mutual relationship of husband and wife. This
is a great mystery, this indeed sets forth the very
mystery that he has been speaking of. "This is a
great mystery: but I speak concerning Christ and
the Church." There you have it. Christ, the
husband; the Church, the wife; Christ, the Head;
the Church, the Body. This is the marvelous mystery that was not made known in other ages, but
has now been fully revealed in the pages of the
New Testament.

Of course we understand that the word "mystery" as used here never means something hard to comprehend. It is not mystery in the sense of being something mysterious and difficult of apprehension. It is rather a sacred secret which the human mind never would have ferreted out, but which awaited divine revelation. In the Old Testament times nobody thought of this wonderful truth, the mystery of Christ and the Church, but it was revealed first to the Apostle Paul and then to others of the New Testament company, and it is the great truth which you and I are called upon to confess and acknowledge in this dispensation of the grace of God.

We are not to be so carried away by the truth back of the marriage relation that we will forget the truth of that relationship between husband and wife. So the apostle drops again from the mystery itself to the commonplace things of life and says, "Nevertheless let every one of you in particular so love his wife even as himself; and the wife see that she reverence her husband." It is such Christian homes as these all over the city, all over the land, that will commend the gospel that is preached from the pulpit. People must see these things lived out in the life, and realize the power of Christ to bind two hearts together and enable them to manifest the mutual relationship of Christ and the Church.

THE CHRISTIAN HOUSEHOLD

✓ ✓ ✓

"Children, obey your parents in the Lord: for this is right. Honor thy father and mother; which is the first commandment with promise; that it may be well with thee, and thou mayest live long on the earth. And, ye fathers, provoke not your children to wrath: but bring them up in the nurture and admonition of the Lord. Servants, be obedient to them that are your masters according to the flesh, with fear and trembling, in singleness of your heart, as unto Christ; not with eyeservice, as men-pleasers; but as the servants of Christ, doing the will of God from the heart; with good will doing service, as to the Lord, and not to men: knowing that whatsoever good thing any man doeth, the same shall he receive of the Lord, whether he be bond or free. And, ye masters, do the same things unto them, forbearing threatening: knowing that your Master also is in heaven; neither is there respect of persons with Him" (Eph. 6: 1-9).

✓ ✓ ✓

IN these nine verses we have the conclusion of that section of the epistle which begins with verse 22 of the previous chapter. We have considered the instruction given to Christian wives and husbands in chapter 5, and have seen that there is to be mutual love, respect, and loyalty, the wife serving in her particular capacity to make the Christian home what it ought to be,

and the husband taking the **responsibility to pro-**
viding for the family, the acknowledged head of
that home seeking to act as in the fear of God—
the wife reverencing her husband, the husband
loving his wife. Now we come to consider other
members of the family, or the same persons in
other relationships.

The apostle speaks first to children. Of course,
he is speaking directly to those who alone really
may be expected to heed the Word of God, to
Christian children. This is one way in which
children may adorn the doctrine of Christ in these
early formative years before they launch out into
the world to make a place for themselves and to
take part in public service for Christ. This is
how they may glorify God and bring honor to the
name of the Lord Jesus Christ. "Children, obey
your parents in the Lord: for this is right." You
see the matter of obedience is put on the common ground of what is correct and proper—"This
is right." You profess to be a Christian, young
man or woman, boy or girl; you have accepted
the Lord Jesus Christ as your Saviour. Well,
then, here is the first admonition He lays upon
you, "Obey your parents." Why? Because it is
the right thing to do. "This is right." In the
Epistle to the Colossians, where you have the
same admonition, he bases it upon another ground.
"Children, obey your parents in all things: for
this is well pleasing unto the Lord" (Col. 3:20).

Do you say sometimes, as some Christian children
do say, "I should like to do some big thing for
Christ; I should like to feel that my life in a
special way is counting for Him?" Well, "this
is well pleasing to the Lord." Obedience, the
recognition of parental authority and loving subjection is well pleasing to Him. In this our
blessed Lord Jesus Christ is our example. We
remember that in Luke 2: 51 we read, "He went
down with them," that is, with His mother, Mary,
and Joseph, his foster father, "and came to
Nazareth, and was subject unto them." Here
you see our blessed Lord Jesus, the eternal Son
of God, become flesh, the example for all Christian
children. What a wonderful thing! If you are a
boy or girl in the home and have trusted the Lord
Jesus, you can say, "My Lord was once a child
like me. He once occupied the same position in
the home that I do and He filled it well. He was
obedient, He was subject to His parents in all
things." The wonder of it is that He, the Creator
of the universe, took that place of subjection,
leaving us an example that we should follow His
steps. Later on as you grow up and go into life
you will have Him as your example in other
spheres, but now He is your example in the home.
How Christian children ought to take this to
heart.

It is a most inconsistent thing for a child to
profess to be a Christian, to have his name on

the roll of some church, to be in fellowship with
an assembly of saints, even partaking of the
sacred supper of the Lord, and yet be characterized by wilfulness and waywardness in the home.
There is nothing more distressing, there is nothing
in some senses more disgusting, than to see a child
who takes the place of a Christian outside and
behaves and acts as anything but one in the private home circle. Disobedience to parents is one
thing about which God's Word speaks most sternly. In Romans 1, where the apostle is describing
the iniquities that prevail in the heathen world,
you will find it linked with the vilest kinds of
sin. In verses 29, 30, we read, "Filled with all
unrighteousness, fornication, wickedness, covetousness, maliciousness; full of envy, murder, de-
bate, deceit, malignity; whisperers, backbiters,
haters of God, despiteful, proud, boasters, in-
ventors of evil things, disobedient to parents."
Notice the place that disobedience to parents has;
it is linked with the vilest immoralities, even with
the crime of homicide, and the reason for it is
that if children are not taught to obey when they
are young, if they do not obey their parents in
the home, they will not obey God, and will not
obey the powers that are ordained of God when
they go out into the world. That judge in Gary,
Indiana, was right who, when recently executing
sentence on some young culprits, said, "I wish it
were possible to put the parents of these children

in the penitentiary for allowing them to grow up like this." As Christian parents we are responsible to see that our children are obedient. And as Christian children we are responsible to obey our parents.

When we turn to Second Timothy we find that the apostle in chapter 3 is describing the outward evidence of the apostasy in the last days, and he again speaks of disobedience to parents as one of the manifest evils of the times. "This know also, that in the last days perilous times shall come. For men shall be lovers of their own selves, covetous, boasters, proud, blasphemers, disobedient to parents, unthankful, unholy" (2 Tim. 3:1). In Romans 1 we have the sins that characterized the heathen world when Christianity began; in Second Timothy 3 we have the sins that will characterize Christendom at the very end immediately before the coming of our Lord Jesus Christ, and you have the same sin emphasized in each case.

Then notice, the apostle draws our attention to the fact that the commandment having special reference to obedience to parents is marked out in a peculiar way. In the Law we read, "Honor thy father and thy mother; that thy days may be long upon the land which the Lord thy God giveth thee" (Exod. 20:21). Read the ten commandments. You see you have four of them with no special promise attached, and then you come to the fifth and you find that God added something.

He added a special promise. It shows the importance that He attaches to obedience to parents.

How important, then, that Christian children should lay this to heart. Do not be content with lip service, do not be content with attending Sunday School and attending the church and young people's meeting, and think that these things constitute Christianity. First learn to show piety at home. It is in the home circle that your life is under closest inspection, and it is there you are called upon to give evidence of a second birth by obedience to your own parents.

Then in verse 4 the apostle speaks to fathers. He does not address himself here particularly to mothers. He says, "Ye fathers, provoke not your children to wrath." You see, it is we fathers who are more inclined to become impatient and unduly harsh and unkind with our children, and yet on the other hand, let me point out that in Hebrews 11, where the Spirit of God is speaking of Moses, exactly the same word that is used here and translated "fathers" is used for Moses' parents. "By faith Moses, when he was born, was hid three months of his parents." The word "parents" there is exactly the same Greek word that is translated "fathers" in Ephesians 6:4. Fathers and mothers are in this sense addressed together, and so the admonition comes home to every one with perhaps peculiar emphasis being placed upon the fathers.

"Ye fathers, provoke not your children to wrath." As Christian parents, have in mind your children's well-being, do not be needlessly demanding of them, do not lay upon them burdens that are too hard for them to bear, for remember, as the children have the Lord Jesus as their example, you have God Himself as yours.

We read, "Like as a father pitieth his children, so the Lord pitieth them that fear Him," and, "If we call Him Father who without respect of persons judgeth according to every man's work," see that you walk circumspectly before Him. Let your attitude toward your children be in accordance with His attitude toward you, and of Him it is written, "He doth not afflict willingly nor grieve the children of men." How we need to take this home to our hearts. "Ye fathers, provoke not your children to wrath;" but bring them up in the nurture and admonition of the Lord, setting them an example of what a Christian should really be, ministering the Word of God to them, praying with them, and walking before them consistently, in the fear of the Lord.

I remember the bitterness with which a young woman, attending a university, came to me and said, "I am in the greatest spiritual distress, and the saddest thing about it is that I cannot consult my own father, who is a minister of the gospel. But I never remember to have heard him lift his voice in prayer with his family, and I never knew

him to gather us about him while he read the
Word of God. He kept all of his religion for the
pulpit, and we never saw any of his piety in the
home." It is in the home we are called first to
manifest godliness, to give prayer and the Word
of God their proper place. Let the grace of
Christ be seen in your life, and though everything
else should go, your children will have the memory
of godly parentage and pious upbringing. What
a sheet-anchor that has been to many young persons launching out in life.

In verse 5, the apostle turns to consider another relationship. He says, "Servants," whether
they be in the home or employees outside. At
the time the apostle wrote, they were slaves, generally speaking. The word *doulos,* translated here
"servants," means slaves, one purchased, but you
notice in verse 8 he is thinking not merely of the
purchased slaves, "Knowing that whatsoever good
thing any man doeth, the same shall he receive
of the Lord, whether he be bond or free." And
therefore the instruction which of old was given
to slaves now applies to all employees. Slaves
were purchased with the money of the master, or
born into the house and raised up by the master,
but today we enter into an agreement, we sell our
labor, and in that way enter into a certain relationship which makes us just as responsible to
heed the admonition given here. There would
never be trouble between capital and labor if the

Word of God were properly revered in this connection, if the instruction given here had proper place in all our hearts and lives. However, it is not expected that unsaved men will heed this admonition, but he is addressing Christian employees. "Servants, be obedient to them that are your masters according to the flesh, with fear and trembling, in singleness of your heart, as unto Christ." That means, of course, the fear of not rendering proper service to your employer, and so of grieving the Holy Spirit of God.

How this dignifies labor! Whether a man be working at the bench, whether one be engaged in the office, whether the miner be down in the bowels of the earth, or the farmer working on the surface of the earth, each may say to himself, "I serve the Lord Christ." When Carey applied for foreign missionary service, somebody said to him, "What is your business?" They intended it as a slur, for he was not a minister. He said, "My business is serving the Lord, and I make shoes to pay expenses." And so every one engaged in any occupation should be able to say, "My business is serving the Lord, and whatever my occupation, that is to pay my expenses, but I am there to serve Him."

"Not with eyeservice, as men-pleasers." I was looking up that word "eyeservice" and found it to be very interesting. It comes from exactly the same word as that translated "servants" in verse

5, and that is, properly speaking, "a slave." Eye-service, then, would be eye-slavery. Did you ever know any one who was an eye-slave? The man who soldiers at his work until somebody says, "The boss is coming!" The young woman who wastes her employer's time until somebody says, "Look out, there is the manager coming through the office," and she immediately gets busy and the typewriter rattles as it has not done for hours. That is eye-slavery. Do not let there be anything like that with the Christians. "Not with eye-service, as men-pleasers; but as the servants of Christ, doing the will of God from the heart." Does not this dignify labor in a wonderful way? No matter what my employment is, I am to do it as unto God from the heart. It is the place in which He has set me and I am there to labor for Him. This lifts me far above all concern about the failure of an employer to properly recognize my worth. When I know I am working for the Lord and He knows everything, it saves from all such thoughts. "Ye are bought with a price; be not ye the servants of men" (1 Cor. 7:23). I may have an employer who does not seem to appreciate me at all, who only wants to get all he can out of me and pay as little as possible, but I have sold my labor to him, and therefore I go on and labor earnestly. I say to myself, "Never mind, there is One who does appreciate, and He knows that I am doing this work in an

upright manner and doing it for His glory, and
some day I shall receive of Him." "Oh, yes, yes,"
you say; "that is all very well. Religion is the
opiate of the people." People of Communistic
tendencies say, "You like to preach resignation to
the poor and tell them that no matter how hard
their lot is here it will be right when they get
to heaven, in order to keep them contented here."
Not at all, that is not what the apostle is saying.
"Be not deceived, God is not mocked, for whatsoever a man soweth that shall he also reap." It
is true in this life as well as in the world to come
that the one who honestly serves the Lord Jesus
Christ is rewarded for it. How many a man
can bear testimony to that! One has labored ap-
parently unappreciated for years until suddenly
under the hand of God circumstances change so
that he is recognized and honored and respected
for what he really is. The Lord sees to this even
in this life, and there is a great deal more coming
in the life ahead.

Now he turns to the masters, Christian masters, again we have to say. "And, ye masters, do
the same things unto them, forbearing threatening: knowing that your Master also is in heaven;
neither is there respect of persons with Him."
"The same things"—you expect your employees
to honor you, to recognize their responsibility to
rightly serve you. Very well, now, masters, it is
your responsibility to properly consider the wel-

fare of your employees; you have been trusted with means or have been put in a position where you administer the means of others—see that you do not look upon your employees as mere "hands," and so much labor to be ground from them, just to get the very most out of them and give the very least; but remember that as they are responsible to serve the Lord Christ, so are you, and you are to do it to His glory.

"Forbearing threatening." Nothing of an unkind, cruel, or discourteous character is to be seen in the Christian master, "Knowing that your Master also is in heaven," and that you have to give an account, therefore, for all your dealings with your employees. If you cut down their wages when it is not necessary, if you seek to force them to work under unhealthful and insanitary conditions, God is looking on and jotting everything down in His books of record when He sees that you behave in an unchristianlike way toward those dependent largely upon you because working for you. See how Christianity equalizes everything. Here is the true socialism, not a leveling of all distinctions, but men and women of every class subject to Christ. That puts everything right. "Ye masters, do the same things unto them, forbearing threatening: knowing that your Master also is in heaven; neither is there respect of persons with Him." Your wealth will not avail if you do not handle it correctly, your place of authority will amount to naught if you do not use it for His glory. "There is no respect of persons with Him." He judgeth according to the works of each one.

What salutary instructions we have here! How important that every Christian, whatever his relationship, should act in accordance with this truth. In the beginning of this epistle we have the highest kind of of spiritual revelation. There it is that we learn that we have been raised up together and seated together in heavenly places in Christ. "Very well," says the apostle, "if you are a heavenly man, a heavenly woman, a member of the Body of Christ, now behave on earth as Christ would if He occupied your position in life, whatever your business may be. Let the Spirit of Christ be manifested in you." This is the thing that will commend Christianity to a lost world.

We have had too much talking of high truth coupled with low living. We have had too much delight in wonderful dispensational unfoldings and yet the truth never affecting the feet. "Order my steps in Thy truth," prays the psalmist. Oh, may God grant that whether as husband or wife, child or parent, employee or employer, we may each one who names the name of Christ manifest His grace in every relationship of life.

If today you are unsaved and you have sometimes stumbled over the inconsistency of Christians, let me say that the Word of God takes it for granted that Christians need constant admonishing, but you are invited to come just as you are to Christ, trust Him as your Saviour, receive the divine life by faith, and then live as a Christian should, and show the rest of us what a real Christian ought to be. Do not be foolish enough to stumble over any one's else inconsistency down to the pit of woe. Remember, there is power to make you what you ought to be, and to make you to be a Christian not in word only but in deed and in truth.

THE CHRISTIAN'S CONFLICT

✦ ✦ ✦

"Finally, my brethren, be strong in the Lord, and in the power of His might. Put on the whole armor of God, that ye may be able to stand against the wiles of the devil. For we wrestle not against flesh and blood, but against principalities, against powers, against the rulers of the darkness of this world, against spiritual wickedness in high places" (Eph. 6: 10-12).

✦ ✦ ✦

WE have already tried to point out the correspondences between this New Testament letter and the Old Testament book of Joshua. We have seen that in the book of Joshua we have the Israelites, a redeemed people, entering upon their possession, the land of Canaan. In the Epistle to the Ephesians we have believers, moved upon by the Spirit of God, entering in possession of that which is now their portion in Christ. We are told of our heavenly inheritance, not merely something which is to be ours when we die and leave this world, or when our blessed Lord comes and summons us to be with Himself, but we are told that here and now we have been blessed "with all spiritual blessings in heavenly places in Christ." There is a grand, a wonderful sphere of blessing which God would have us enter into in spirit while we are in this world as to the body.

A great many people are accustomed to think of Canaan as representing only heaven after death, and therefore they think of the river Jordan as always representing death itself. If you will stop and think for a moment, you will realize that there is a sense in which Canaan could scarcely represent the heaven to which we are going in all its fulness, because it was after the people of Israel entered that land that their real conflict began. They found it was already tenanted by hostile nations who immediately rushed to arms to withstand the people of Israel, and who sought to keep them from the enjoyment of that which God had given them. When you and I who are saved are finally called away from this world, we are not going to the other side for conflict, we shall not find ourselves engaged in battle with evil spirits in heaven. But as believers in the Lord Jesus Christ, when we seek here on earth to appropriate the blessings that are already ours in Him, we find at once that there is a host of evil powers seeking to keep us out of the experience of these precious things. Therefore, we can see how Canaan represents primarily our present place of blessing in the heavenlies. The armies of Canaan, disputing Israel's possession, represent what we have here in verse 12, the principalities and powers, the world-rulers of this darkness, who are doing their utmost to keep Christians living on a low, worldly level, and thus failing to enjoy the victory that is theirs by right because of their relationship to the Lord Jesus Christ.

We have considered the Christian home and the Christian household, and reading those precious verses we found ourselves in an atmosphere of peace and blessing such as the unconverted know nothing of. When Paul wrote this letter, there were very few Christian homes in the world, but, thank God, as a result of the proclamation of the truth during nineteen centuries, all over this and other lands may be found homes that answer to what we have here in Ephesians—homes where husband and wife together are seeking to glorify the Lord Jesus Christ, each giving honor to the other, each seeking to fulfil his or her place in the economy of the family, and where the children are growing up in the nurture and admonition of the Lord, where masters and servants alike recognize their responsibility to the great Master in heaven who was once a Servant here on earth.

It is very striking that as we turn from the beautiful description of the Christian household we immediately find ourselves in an altogether different atmosphere. The apostle has barely concluded his admonition to husband and wife, parents and children, masters and servants, before he speaks of warfare and conflict; for we cannot always enjoy the sweetness and quietness of a Christian home. We have to go out into the world, we have to go out into life, there to meet cruel enemies on every hand who seek to disrupt and destroy our Christian experience and endeavor in every possible way to lead us to do or say things that will bring dishonor on the name of our blessed Lord. We go from the home to the battle-field.

We are reminded, as the apostle closes his letter, that we are not yet in heaven, we have not reached the rest that remains for the people of God, and therefore he says, "Finally, my brethren, be strong in the Lord, and in the power of His might." Perhaps it might be rendered, "My brethren, be daily strengthened," for it is in the continuous tense; be constantly receiving strength from the Lord and go forth in the power of His might. It is important to realize that even after we have been converted for many years we have no more power in ourselves to insure victory over the foe than we had when first saved. The excellency of the power is not in us but in God, and therefore the necessity of living in communion with Him. The preacher cannot do his work aright unless in communion with God, the choir cannot sing aright, the workman at his bench or machine cannot do his work aright and bring glory to the name of the Lord Jesus Christ, the young woman at her desk, the man selling goods upon the street, the farmer at the plow, cannot work aright unless in communion with God. We all need His mighty quickening power to enable us to triumph in our respective spheres just as much as any missionary going to a foreign field to carry the gospel to lost men and women. Here is a challenge to everyone of us. We must face it for we cannot overcome in our own strength, therefore the importance of living near to the Lord, being strengthened in the Lord and in the power of His might.

"Put on the whole armor of God, that ye may be able to stand against the wiles of the devil." This is the armor that we have delineated for us piece by piece in the next section of the epistle. But the armor is of God, it is nothing of ourselves, for we have nothing in ourselves whereby we can meet the foe. "Put on the whole armor of God, that ye may be able to stand against the wiles of the devil." It is not only here but in other scriptures as well that the apostle by the Spirit insists upon this. In Romans 13:11 we read, "And that, knowing the time, that now it is high time to awake out of sleep: for now is our salvation nearer than when we believed. The night is far spent, the day is at hand . . . let us walk honestly, as in the day; not in rioting and drunkenness, not in chambering and wantonness, not in strife and envying. But put ye on the Lord Jesus Christ, and make not provision for the flesh, to fulfil the lusts thereof." How many a Christian has forgotten words like these, and forgetting them has found himself absolutely powerless in the hour of temptation, unarmed, exposed to every imagination of a cruel foe. "Put on the whole armor of God."

Then again, in 2 Corinthians 10, the apostle speaks of this same warfare. He tells us that it is not a conflict with the flesh. We are not told to fight the flesh but to reckon ourselves dead to sin in the flesh. Our conflict is with the fallen spirits that dominate this present age of evil. These spirits, of course, cannot indwell believers, but they can do a great deal in the way of alluring believers into by-paths where they bring dishonor to the name of the Lord. In verses 3-5 we read, "For though we walk in the flesh, we do not war against the flesh: for the weapons of our warfare are not carnal, but mighty through God to the pulling down of strongholds. Casting down imaginations [or human reason, for Satan works through the mind, getting men to reason rather than to believe what God has revealed in His Holy Word], and every high thing that exalteth itself against the knowledge of God, and bringing into captivity every thought to the obedience of Christ." Here, then, is our conflict. We are exposed to these evil spirits who are haters of God and of our blessed Saviour and therefore seek to bring dishonor upon the Lord, upon that holy Name whereby we are called, by leading us off into things that grieve the Holy Spirit and bring discredit upon our testimony. How needful then the admonition, "Put on the whole armor of God, that ye may be able to stand against the wiles of the devil."

It would be a very simple thing if the adversary of our souls came to us honestly and said, "Good morning. I am the devil, and I want you to get into something that is going to cause you a lot of misery and wretchedness, and which will dishonor your Saviour; and if you will only listen to me and obey me, I will be able to accomplish this." We would have no difficulty in saying to him, "Get thee behind me, Satan: for thou savorest not the things that be of God, but the things that be of men" (Mark 8:33). But he does not come that way. He is transformed into an angel of light, and he seeks to deceive us. Here we read of the *wiles* of the devil. The word, "wile," is the very one from which we get our English word "method," but it implies a subtle method or craftiness. He is an old campaigner; he has been at the business of deceiving men and women for at least six millenniums, and he knows exactly how to approach every individual soul as he comes with his crafty method. You get an illustration of that in the book of Joshua.

God had told Joshua to cross over Jordan and that he would find there the seven nations of Canaan. They were corrupt and abominable, given to all kinds of vileness and idolatry, and the

Israelites were commanded not to enter into any leagues or marriages with them, but to destroy them utterly. The words were plain, and for a time Joshua and the people carried them out implicitly. But one day there came a strange-looking group of men limping up the highway, dressed in rags. They had worn sandals on their feet, and carried on their arms old sacks which contained moldy bread. Their goat-skin water-bottles were cracked and dried up. Some of Joshua's scouts went out to see them and asked, "Who are you, and what do you want?"

"We would like to see your general," they said.

And so they were led into the presence of Joshua, and he inquired, "Well, what is it you want with us? Where do you come from?"

"From a very far country," they said. "You see these clothes of ours. They were brand-new the day we left home and you can realize that we have come a long way. These sandals were bought from the shoe-dealer the day we left. This bread was brought fresh from the oven, but now it is all moldy. We have come a long distance because we have heard of you and of how God is with you. We would like to make an alliance with you. Let us be friends. We would be very proud to be linked up with you, and we hope that you will be willing to make an alliance with us."

"This is most interesting," said Joshua; "you

say you are from a long way off. How did you hear about us?"

"Oh, the word is going all through the land. We heard of the victory as you entered the land, how Jericho and Ai fell before you. Let us get together and make an alliance."

And we read that the men made a league with them and asked not counsel of the Lord. Thus they were deceived by the wiles of the Gibeonites. A day or two after they had made the league, when there was no chance to break it, they found out that these men came from a nearby village and were anxious to link up with them in order to save their own lives. How the devil has wrought along that line through the years! One of his first attempts to corrupt the Church of God is by getting unconverted people into its fellowship. Today the membership of churches is largely made up of unsaved men and women. When it comes to public service for the Lord, one of the great abominations in the church today is that of unconverted people joining together in a choir to professedly sing the praises of the Lord. Choir-members who are flirting with the world are just as truly a hindrance to the work of God as the preacher flirting with the world. It is one of the wiles of the devil to try to mix the saved and the unsaved together. Of course there is no blessing when such a condition exists. Oh, to be out and out for God!

We are to stand against the wiles of the devil, recognizing this, that we wrestle not against flesh and blood. We have no quarrel with men, no fight with our fellow-beings, we are not wrestling with flesh and blood but against principalities and powers. These are the principalities of fallen angels who are marshaled under the skull and cross-bones banner of the devil himself. "Against principalities, against powers, against the rulers of the darkness of this world, against spiritual wickedness in high places." It might be translated, "Against the world-rulers of this darkness." Who are the world-rulers of this darkness? They are the great evil powers, evil angels, who are seeking to control the hearts of those in authoritative positions in the world, to hinder men and women from subjecting themselves to the truth of God. Take the last great world conflict. Who were the rulers of the world? "Well," you say, "there was President Wilson, King George of England, Kaiser Wilhelm of Germany, King Victor Emmanuel of Italy." No, they were not the actual rulers of the world; they were simply like the pawns upon the chess-board. The world-rulers were the wicked spirits endeavoring to influence the hearts of men and move them for the destruction of the human race. So malignant is the spirit of these evil beings spoken of here in the Word of God that we are not competent to meet them; we cannot face foes like these and come forth victorious save as we put on the whole armor of God, save as we draw our strength day by day from our blessed Lord Himself, and as we use the sword of the Spirit which is the Word of God.

When we get home to heaven our conflict will be over. But you ask, "Do we not read of conflict there?" In Revelation 12 we read: "Michael and his angels fought against the dragon; and the dragon fought and his angels, and prevailed not; neither was their place found any more in heaven. And the great dragon was cast out, that old serpent, called the Devil, and Satan, which deceiveth the whole world: he was cast out into the earth, and his angels were cast out with him." You see when we go up, he, the mighty foe who throughout the centuries has been the accuser of the people of God, comes down. But our conflict is while we are still in this world. I am afraid a great many Christians never realize this; they never stop to think that day by day Satan and his hosts are doing their very best to keep them from honoring the Lord Jesus, to keep them from prayer, to keep them from the study of the Word, to bring into their lives something that will bring discredit on the Saviour's name, and consequently we see today a largely divided Church simply because believers do not know what our conflict is. "We wrestle not against flesh and blood, but against principalities, against powers, against the rulers of the darkness of this world, against spiritual wickedness in high places."

Note that last expression, "Against spiritual wickedness in high places." It seems as though the translators of our beautiful Authorized Version hardly dared accept what this passage really teaches, although they have put in the margin the rendering that makes it clear. It is, "Against wicked spirits in heavenly places." It is an altogether wrong thought that Satan and his hosts are already confined in hell. Quite the contrary is true; they are still in the heavenly places. That does not mean that they are in the immediate presence of God. In Scripture, we have three heavens: the heaven where the birds fly, the atmosphere; and then the stellar heaven; and beyond all that the heaven of heavens, the third heaven, the immediate presence of God. Satan and his hosts are represented in Scripture as in the lower heavens. The devil is "the prince of the power of the air." And inasmuch as the eyes of the Lord are everywhere, he is pictured as in the very presence of God as the accuser of the brethren. Our conflict is with these wicked spirits.

We may well sing:

> "A charge to keep I have,
>   A God to glorify,
> A never-dying soul to save,
>   And fit it for the sky."

We have been saved as far as deliverance from the guilt of our sin is concerned, but we are now to be saved practically by conformity to Christ and subjection to the Word of God, that thus we may be fitted in the fullest possible sense for fellowship with Him. May God give us to be on our guard, to remember that we cannot put the sword out of our hand, that we cannot rest upon past victories as long as we are in this scene. "Let him that thinketh he standeth take heed lest he fall." And yet there is no reason for discouragement because, as our faith and trust is centered in Christ, we may know that "greater is He that is in you than he that is in the world."

THE WHOLE ARMOR OF GOD

✓ ✓ ✓

"Wherefore take unto you the whole armor of God, that ye may be able to withstand in the evil day, and having done all, to stand. Stand therefore, having your loins girt about with truth and having on the breastplate of right-eousness; and your feet shod with the preparation of the gospel of peace; above all, taking the shield of faith, where-with ye shall be able to quench all the fiery darts of the wicked. And take the helmet of salvation, and the sword of the Spirit, which is the Word of God: praying always" (Eph. 6: 13-18).

✓ ✓ ✓

AS we have considered the Christian's conflict we have found that it is not with flesh and blood, nor is it with our own carnal nature, for we have not been called upon to fight with that but simply to deny it, to refuse its claims. It is a conflict with the wicked spirits in the heavenlies who would seek to keep us from the blessed enjoyment of our portion in Christ. This they do in many insidious ways as well as by open manifestations of warfare. We are to stand against the wiles of the devil, for in every conceivable manner he will seek to hinder us from making progress in our Christian lives, in our Christian experience, and therefore, we need to be constantly upon the watch and we need to be accoutered with the whole armor of God.

"Wherefore take unto you the whole armor of God." This is something very different from the garments in which we stand before God through grace. Every one of us who have put our trust in the Lord Jesus Christ has been made the righteousness of God in Him, the best robe is his. We stand before God in Christ, but we do not put this on ourselves. God has clothed us. But when it comes to the panoply for conflict, we need to put on each separate piece of armor in order to withstand in the evil days when the hosts of hell are pressing upon our souls and it seems as though we would be borne down and defeated. We are not to turn our backs and flee from the foe. We are not to act on the presumption that "he who fights and runs away may live to fight another day," but we are to face the foe, for there is no armor for the back. If we turn our backs, if we retreat, we but expose ourselves to the fiery darts of the wicked one, but as we face the foe unflinchingly in the power of the finished work of Calvary we shall be able to stand.

"And having done all, to stand." Where and how do we stand? Is it simply by determination of our own, in some goodness of our own? Not at all. But we stand in the perfection of Christ's finished work. The foe cannot harm us there. We meet the foe in the name of Christ, the Victor. We claim victory over him because of the One who has already defeated him on the cross. There Satan bruised the heel of our blessed, divine Redeemer, but his own head was bruised also, and now we are entitled to consider the devil as one already defeated. But, though he knows he is defeated and that his doom is sure, he will do everything he can to harass and distress the Christian as long as he is in this scene. Therefore the need of standing strong in faith, resisting the devil in the power of the cross of Christ.

"Stand therefore, having your loins girt about with truth." That may seem to us Occidentals a somewhat awkward expression. There would be no question in the mind of an Oriental, for he wears long flowing garments in which he is perfectly comfortable when just moving about at leisure; but if going on a journey or engaged in any kind of conflict, he must draw them up about his waist, holding them in by a girdle, so as not to impede his efforts or hinder progress. Just so, you and I as believers are to have our loins girt about with truth. What does he mean? Elsewhere we read, "Gird up therefore the loins of your minds." Just as the Orientals' flowing garments are to be rightly girded that they may not be carried about by the wind, so we are to have

the loins of our minds girt about with truth in
order that our imaginations may not be "carried
about by every wind of doctrine, by the sleight
of men, and cunning craftiness, whereby they lie
in wait to deceive." We are to gird up, to draw
up, the loins of our minds, "bringing every
thought into captivity to the obedience of Christ."
In other words, our minds are to be controlled by
what God has spoken, not by what we think.

I wish Christians would come back to the Book.
I am often distressed when people ask me, "What
do you think about this, or what do you think
about that?" And I have to tell them, "It does
not make any difference what I think. My
thoughts do not amount to anything. The great
question is, What has God said? What is written
in the Word?" If the Word does not speak, we
have no right to attempt to speak, but where it
has given a clear definite declaration, we should
be positive and sure in our faith. That is what
it is to have the loins of the mind girt about with
the truth of God, our thoughts all brought into
subjection to His Holy Word. How important
that is when you have to face the devil, because
he works through wily error, presenting all kinds
of false systems and views and evil-speaking in
regard to Christ. It is only as our minds are
controlled by the Word that we will be able to
meet these things. The better you know the Bible,
the better fitted you are to meet the assaults of

the enemy, and yet some of you have never even
read your Bible through once. Have you? You
have never gotten beyond the genealogies. You
came right up against them and stopped. You
never went any farther. You did not know that
hidden in those genealogical chapters there are
some of the most beautiful little gems you will
find anywhere in the Bible. You will miss them
if you are not careful.

A friend of mine used to tell of listening to
Andrew Bonar many years ago. Dr. Bonar was
speaking on heaven and the great reunion of loved
ones over there, and in his eloquent way he pictured the believer newly come from earth walking
along the golden street and suddenly coming right
up against a group of Old Testament sages and
prophets. In a moment he recognizes them and
says, "Why, this is Ezekiel; isn't it?"

"Yes," says Ezekiel, "I am so glad to meet
you."

"And this is Micah and Zechariah and Amos."

And then Andrew Bonar said, "And just imagine Ezekiel saying, 'Oh, you knew about me;
did you? How did you like the book I wrote?'

'Book? What book was that?'

'Oh, surely you remember my book! Did you
enjoy it?'

'I am sorry to say I never read it.'

"And then Micah would say, 'And what did
you think of my book?'

'Let me see; was that in the Old Testament or in the New Testament? It seems to me I remember there was such a book.'

"How would you feel to have to meet these men when you never have read their books?"

Some of you had better get busy. There is far too much time spent in reading novels and in reading the newspapers and too little time given to the Word of God. Good literature is fine, reading the newspaper is all right, but these things should not crowd out time for reading God's Word.

There was an old Scotchman who could neither read nor write. His minister wanted to teach him and so, although he was very busy, he arranged to go to this man's house for an hour every day and teach him. He took the Gospel of John as a text-book, and the old Scot was greatly interested. By-and-by the minister was called away for a time, and when he came back he wanted to see how his pupil was progressing. He went to his home, but the man was not there. The minister asked the wife how her husband was getting along with his reading. "Oh," she said, "he is doing very well."

"Is he able to read now?"

"Yes, he is doing wonderfully."

"Is he able to enjoy the reading of his Bible?"

"Oh," she said, "he has gotten away out of the Bible and into the newspaper long ago."

Remember, the Bible is the only Book that will last for all eternity, and anything you get out of it here you will have for all the ages to come.

And then we are to have on "the breastplate of righteousness." I want you to follow me carefully here, for sometimes I have difficulty in making this verse clear to people. It is a blessed truth that we have been made the righteousness of God in Christ. It is a wonderful thing to know that righteousness is imputed instead of sin to every believer in the Lord Jesus; but that is not the righteousness referred to here. You see, you and I do not put on the righteousness of God. God does that for us. But here is something we are to put on. Turn back to Isaiah 59, the portion that the apostle evidently had in mind. You will see that the righteousness referred to is practical righteousness. "And he saw that there was no man, and wondered that there was no intercessor: therefore His arm brought salvation unto Him; and His righteousness, it sustained Him. For He put on righteousness as a breastplate, and an helmet of salvation upon His head; and He put on the garments of vengeance for clothing and was clad with zeal as a cloke" (Isa. 59: 16, 17). Isaiah speaks here of the Messiah, our blessed Lord. He put on righteousness as a breastplate. That is something different from what was always His in eternity. He came into this world as a Man, and, as a man, was obedient in all things to the will of God. He put on righteousness as a breastplate, and now you and I are called to imitate Him by putting on the breastplate of righteousness.

The breastplate covers the heart of the man, and when we think of the heart we think of the conscience; and mark this, unless you as a Christian keep a good conscience in regard to practical living, you will never be able to defeat your foe. When the devil comes against you and you know there is some hidden sin in your life, you will go down, you will not be able to stand against him. How many a one has failed when Satan made a tremendous assault upon him, and people said, "Wasn't it sad?—such a failure and coming so suddenly." But it was not suddenly, for there had been an undermining going on weeks and months and perhaps years, little unrighteousnesses indulged in here and there, unholy thoughts, wicked things going on that were not dealt with in the presence of God; and when the foe came there was an exposed breast because righteousness had not been put on as the breastplate. Go to deal with the unsaved, and if they know that you do not have on the breastplate of righteousness, your testimony will not amount to very much. You may say to a friend, "I would like you to come to meeting with me," and he may say to you, "I don't know, Jack; but it doesn't seem to have done very much for you." He has preached on a text, if you ever dare to stand up before an audience when you go to preach the Word without getting your message fresh from the living God and going out in confidence in Him instead of in yourself, you will be a failure. I want that lesson to be impressed upon my own heart, that is why I am putting it so strongly to you. "Having the shield of faith, wherewith ye shall be able to quench all the fiery darts of the wicked."

Now there is something for our heads. "And take the helmet of salvation." That is, if I have any doubt as to my own salvation, I will have no real confidence when it comes to facing the foe. Therefore, for a helmet, I take the knowledge of salvation that He has given through His Word.

Then we read, "And the sword of the Spirit, which is the Word of God." Do not make a mistake here; the sword of the Spirit is not the Bible. This Bible is not the sword of the Spirit, it is the armory. There are thousands of swords in here and every one of them is powerful and two-edged. There are two different terms in Greek for "word." There is *"logos,"* which is the term we usually use, but the other word, *"rhema,"* is the one used here. It means, "a saying." "And the sword of the Spirit, which is the saying of God." If the devil comes and you throw the Bible at him, it is not going to drive him away. You might do that, and go down yourself. But when he comes, and you say, "Here is what God says," and you have a definite saying of God to meet the case, you defeat him. Take the example of the blessed Lord in the wilderness. The devil came so cunningly and said, "If Thou be the Son of God, command that these stones be made bread." Jesus answered, "It is written, Man shall not live by bread alone, but by every word that proceedeth out of the mouth of God." He took the sword out of the armory. You need to know your Bible so that you will be able to meet the devil whenever he comes with these suggestions. Then the devil showed Jesus all the kingdoms of the world, and said, "All these things will I give Thee, if Thou wilt fall down and worship me." Out came another sword and the Lord went at the devil with it. He replied, "It is written, Thou shalt worship the Lord thy God, and Him only shalt thou serve." Then the devil tried to use the saying of God himself. He took Jesus up on a pinnacle of the temple and said, "It is written, He shall give His angels charge concerning Thee: and in their hands they shall bear Thee up, lest at any time Thou dash Thy foot against a stone." Think of the effrontery of the devil quoting Scripture, and that to the Lord of life and glory Himself! But he left out the most important part of the verse. It reads, "For He shall give His angels charge over Thee, to keep Thee in all Thy ways. They shall bear Thee up in their hands, lest Thou dash Thy foot against a stone." The Son of God was not falling from the temple in order that men should see Him borne up by angel hands. That was not part of "His ways." The Lord used another "saying" from the Book of God; He said, "It is written again, Thou shalt not tempt the Lord thy God." The sword of the Spirit is the saying of God. Get to know your Bible, and then when the devil comes against you, you will be able to say, "But the Book says thus and so," and you will have the Word for him.

If we want the blessing of God, we must walk in obedience to His blessed Word.

But now after all this, when you have the various parts of the armor in place, there is something that must never be omitted. Bunyan speaks of it as actually a part of the armor. He says, "In addition to all the rest there was a piece called 'all prayer.'" "Praying always with all prayer and supplication in the Spirit." You see, the armored believer is independent of the devil because he is utterly dependent upon God, and prayer is the source of his dependence. But we must consider this more fully in our next chapter.

PRAYER AND SUPPLICATION IN THE HOLY SPIRIT

✱ ✱ ✱

"Praying always with all prayer and supplication in the Spirit, and watching thereunto with all perseverance and supplication for all saints; and for me, that utterance may be given unto me, that I may open my mouth boldly, to make known the mystery of the gospel, for which I am an ambassador in bonds; that therein I may speak boldly, as I ought to speak. But that ye also may know my affairs, and how I do, Tychicus, a beloved brother and faithful minister in the Lord, shall make known to you all things: whom I have sent unto you for the same purpose, that ye might know our affairs, and that he might comfort your hearts. Peace be to the brethren, and love with faith, from God the Father and the Lord Jesus Christ. Grace be with all them that love our Lord Jesus Christ in sincerity. Amen" (Eph. 6: 18-24).

✱ ✱ ✱

WE have been considering the armor of the Christian soldier. We have noticed that he is to put on the breastplate of practical righteousness, that he is to have his feet shod with the preparation of the gospel of peace. In other words, his walk is to be in accordance with the gospel. Then in the third place, he is to have his loins girt about with truth, and, fourth, he is to take the shield of faith, of confidence in God wherewith to quench the fiery darts of the foe. On his head he is to have the helmet of salvation, for no one can go forth with boldness to meet Satan and his cohorts unless he has the assurance of his own salvation through the finished work of Christ. Then he is to have in his hand the sword of the Spirit, which is not merely the Word of God in the sense that the Bible is the Word, but, as we have seen, the "saying" of God. He is to know his Bible so well that he can draw from this blessed armory the particular saying that he needs at a given moment. In addition to this, he is to keep the line of communication between himself and his God clear.

Some of you remember that during the late World War a regiment went into the Argonne Forest and was lost. For days they were out of touch with headquarters and we were reading about the "lost regiment." When at last they were located, their ranks had been sadly decimated. When a Christian in the conflict with Satan gets out of touch with headquarters, it is a terrible thing. The apostle, after indicating the various pieces of armor, says, "Praying always with all prayer and supplication in the Spirit." The trouble with many of us is that we pray only when we get into difficulty, when times are hard and circumstances are going against us. Then we remember the Word, "Call upon Me in the day of trouble: I will deliver thee, and thou shalt glorify Me" (Ps. 50: 15). But we would be spared a great many of our troubles if we continued instant in prayer; if, when everything was going well with us, we were just as faithful about the hour of prayer as when things were going against us. "Praying always with all prayer."

God declares in His Word that He will not hear the prayer of the wicked. It is an abomination to the Lord, and David says, "If I regard iniquity in my heart, the Lord will not hear me." But if I have judged all known sin and have on the breastplate of righteousness, I am in that attitude, that position, where I can pray in confidence. "All prayer" is an approach to God, but note the added word, "supplication." This suggests definite petition. It is one thing to approach God in prayer with a heart full of praise and thanksgiving and in a general way commit one's affairs to Him. It is another thing to come with a very definite supplication for a particular matter, for special trouble at a given time. We read, "Be careful for nothing; but in everything by prayer and supplication"—there you have the same word again, it is prayer and petition—"with thanksgiving, let your requests be made known unto God. And the peace of God, which passeth all understanding, shall keep your hearts and minds through Christ Jesus" (Phil. 4: 6, 7). No difficulty that I have to face is too great for God, and nothing that troubles me is too insignificant for His care.

Arthur T. Pierson sat with George Mueller one day, and Mr. Mueller was telling him of some of the wonderful things that God had done for the orphanage at Bristol. As he talked he was writing, and Dr. Pierson noticed that he was having difficulty with his pen-point. Right in the midst of the conversation Mr. Mueller seemed to lose sight of his visitor, he bowed his head for a moment or two in prayer, and then began writing again. Mr. Pierson said, "Mr. Mueller, what were you praying about just now?" "Oh," Mr. Mueller said, "perhaps you didn't notice that I was having trouble with this pen-point. I haven't another, and this is an important letter, so I was asking the Lord to help me so that I could write it clearly." "Dear me," said Dr. Pierson, "a man who trusts God for millions of pounds also prays about a scratchy pen-point." Yes, you may go to Him about everything.

Then notice, it is "prayer and supplication in the Spirit." And that may check many of us when it comes to the hour of prayer. Prayer in the Spirit is prayer in accordance with the mind of the indwelling Holy Spirit of God. No unconverted person, of course, can pray in the Spirit, but there are even Christians who are in such a low carnal condition of soul that it is impossible for them to pray in the Spirit. I cannot pray in the Spirit if I am harboring a grudge against my brother. I cannot pray in the Spirit if there is

anyone I will not forgive because of some real
or fancied wrong done to me. I cannot pray in
the Spirit if I have a selfish motive, if I am
seeking merely my own glory or comfort. I cannot pray in the Spirit if I have a covetous heart.

You remember the Apostle James says, "Ye
ask and receive not, because ye ask amiss, that
ye may consume it upon your lusts" (James 4: 3).
I can pray in the Spirit only as I am walking in
the Spirit, as I am living in the Spirit. Then He,
the blessed Third Person of the Trinity, who
dwells in every believer, will guide my thoughts
aright as I come to God in prayer. Very often
one goes to God about certain things when in an
unspiritual state, only to find out when restored
to fellowship that he would be better far without
them, and so he no longer asks for them. In the
Old Testament we read, "Delight thyself also in
the Lord, and He shall give thee the desires of
thine heart." If I am really delighting myself in
the Lord, I will want only those things which
will glorify God, I will not be asking from a selfish viewpoint. I shall want God to do for me
that which will magnify Christ in my life and
make Him more precious to my soul.

"Praying always with all prayer and supplication in the Spirit, and watching thereunto with
all perseverance." "Watch and pray," our Lord
Jesus Christ said, "lest ye enter into temptation,"
and this, of course, only emphasizes what we have

seen already. If I would pray aright, I must live aright, and so I am to watch against anything that would come into my life to grieve the Spirit of God and thus hinder real prayer.

Then, observe, the Lord would not have me concerned only with my own affairs. He says, "And supplication for all saints." A brother beloved said to me the other day, "For years my interests have largely been in the work in which I myself was engaged, or in connection with certain institutions in which I had a part, but I find the Lord is drawing me in these days to think of His work everywhere, and of His people in every place." This surely is an evidence of growth in grace. We are so inclined to narrow down our thoughts to our own little circles. We may not pray in the same way as the man who said, "God bless me, and my wife, our son John, and his wife. Us four, and no more," but we do pray most earnestly for those connected intimately with us. We should do this, but in addition let us consider the whole Church of God; let us think of all His beloved people in every place, and bear them up in the arms of our faith and love. If in this way we go to God, we will never lack subjects about which to speak to Him.

Some years ago I was visiting a very devoted company of Christians in a western State. They had some rather peculiar ideas. They came together weekly to study the Bible, and for preaching, and remembering the Lord in observing His Supper, but they had no prayer-meeting. I said to them, "Do you never have a prayer-meeting?"

A brother said, "Oh, no; we have nothing to pray for."

"How is that?" I asked.

"Why, God has blessed us 'with all spiritual blessings in heavenly places in Christ,' so we do not need to pray for spiritual blessings. We do not need to pray for temporal blessings, for we have everything we need. We are well cared for; we have all the land we know how to till. We do not need to pray for money, for we have plenty to keep us going. We do not need to pray for wives, for we are all married. We do not need to pray for children; I have thirteen, and Brother So-and-So has fifteen. We have nothing to pray for, so we just give God thanks."

"My dear brother," I said, "I wish, if for nothing else, you would come together to pray for me."

"We can do that at home," he said. "If we came together to pray we wouldn't have anything to say."

"But what about the word, 'And supplication for all saints?' Suppose you do nothing else but come together to remind one another of the Lord's dear children that you know, and spend an hour telling God about them."

But he did not see it. They seemed to have no idea of what prayer really is. Sometime after that I was in Minneapolis. One day I tumbled over, and when I came to I had a fever of one hundred and four degrees. I was on my back with typhoid fever for six weeks. When at last, a year later, I got out to that same section, they said to me, "When we got word that you were so very sick, we had two prayer-meetings a week to pray for you, and our hearts were greatly burdened, but as soon as we got word that you were well enough to go home again, we stopped." "Why did you stop?" I asked. "When flat on my back, I did not have any trouble with the devil, but when strong and well and I have to go out to face the foe, I need prayer far more." He looked at me in amazement and said, "I never thought of it in that way." The Apostle Paul himself not only exhorted saints to pray for one another, but he said, "And for me, that utterance may be given unto me, that I may open my mouth boldly." I am sure that those of us who stand on public platforms and preach Christ will never know until we get to heaven how much we owe to the prayers of God's hidden ones. It has often come like a benediction when some dear saint, possibly a shut-in, writes to me and says, "My dear brother, daily in prayer I remember you and the work that God has given you to do." How much it means to know that all over this and other lands there

are prayer-helpers who are crying to God, "Keep
that brother from blundering, keep him from sin."
There are temptations on every hand, and how
much the man who stands in the pulpit needs
divine help that he may be kept from anything
that would mar his testimony.

"Pray," says the apostle, "for me, that utterance may be given me, that I may open my mouth
boldly, to make known the mystery of the gospel."
Sometimes God's dear children are far more
ready with criticism of preachers than they are
with prayer for them. They say, "Well, I don't
know; but Mr. ———— doesn't seem to me to have
much power, he doesn't seem to have much gift,
he doesn't seem to make things very clear." And
I often feel like saying, "Do you ever pray for
him that he may have power, that he may have
clarity to so preach the truth that men and women
will believe?"

In Acts 14:1 we read that the apostles "so
spake that a great multitude believed," which implies that one may so speak that no one will believe. What is needed is not only the word of the
preacher, but that message backed up by the
prayers of the people of God. It is a blessed thing
to know that one is being borne up by the saints
in prayer. Paul valued this, and he was the
greatest of all the apostles in his ministry. I am
sure that at the judgment-seat of Christ, when
our blessed Lord is giving a reward to the Apostle

Paul, He will call up many of the saints of whom we have never heard and have them stand with Paul, for they were his fellow-helpers in his ministry, and He will say, "You held up his hands in prayer, and you must share in the reward."

He speaks of making known "the mystery of the gospel." This does not mean that it is something hard to understand, but it is a divine secret that man would never have guessed if God Himself had not made it known. One reason why I am absolutely certain that the gospel is of God is, that no man left to himself would ever have dreamed of telling us that God became Man to save us from our sins. All human religions take the opposite viewpoint. They try to tell us how man may save himself and eventually obtain a position akin to the Godhead. But not one of them tells us that God became Man to save us from our sins. This is the mystery of the gospel, the divine secret that we are called upon to proclaim to men.

"I am an ambassador in bonds." What a remarkable declaration! The ambassador from the court of St. James comes to Washington and has his many medals and decorations on him, but here the ambassador of the highest court of heaven says, "Do you want to see my decorations?" And he points to his fetters and says, "I am an ambassador in chains." Somebody has well said, "God is not going to look us over for medals and

decorations but for scars, to see what we have
endured for Christ's sake." He was a suffering,
afflicted, jailed ambassador, and he says, "Pray
for me, that I may speak boldly, as I ought to
speak." And right there in the prison he wit-
nessed for Christ. The very soldiers who were
guarding him heard the story of salvation. We
read in another of his epistles, "All the saints
salute you, chiefly they that are of Caesar's
guard." Our Authorized Version says, "Caesar's
household," but he is not talking about Caesar's
butler and baker and candlestick-maker, but of
his soldiers. They probably were heathen when
set to guard him, but Christians before they got
through with him. He preached the mystery of
the gospel to them and their souls were saved.
How much of that was in answer to prayer we
will never know until the books are opened in
that day.

In the next two verses he gives us the only personal word in the epistle in which he names any
one else other than himself and the Lord. "But
that ye also may know my affairs, and how I do,
Tychicus, a beloved brother and faithful minister
in the Lord, shall make known to you all things:
whom I have sent unto you for the same purpose,
that ye might know our affairs, and that he might
comfort your hearts." In Acts 20:4 we read of
Tychicus. He was an Asian. Ephesus was in
Asia, and probably Tychicus was well-known to

these brethren, so **Paul** sent him back in order to give a report as to how things were going with him. Notice the language he uses concerning him, "A beloved brother and faithful minister in the Lord." In Colossians 4: 7 he says, "All my state shall Tychicus declare unto you, who is a beloved brother and a faithful minister and fellow-servant in the Lord." Tychicus must have been a very delightful man to meet. It is not often the two things are combined in one man— beloved and faithful. Generally your beloved brother is so gracious and gentle and easy-going that everybody likes him because he does not find fault with anyone, and they say, "Isn't he nice?" It is like the lady who, after she had listened to a Scotch preacher, was asked, "What did you think of the sermon? Wasn't it beautiful?" "Yes, it was beautiful," she said; "but it wouldn't hurt a flea." They like the preacher who does not hurt anybody, who draws beautiful word-pictures, etc., and who never reproves sin. "A good mixer," they call him today. That is the very thing Paul said we were not to be. "Come out from among them, and be ye separate." But as a rule they are the beloved kind. On the other hand, the faithful brother is apt to be so rigid that he gets a little bit legal, and goes around clubbing this one and that one, and saying, "I don't care what people think of me; I am going to be faithful." He is rather disagreeable, you know. You do not like to get too close to men like that. But Tychicus combined in himself the beloved pastor and the faithful exhorter. That is a wonderful combination, too high for most of us to attain to.

And then in verses 23, 24 we have the closing words. You will observe there are no personal salutations in Ephesians. The reason probably was that the Epistle to the Ephesians was a circular letter, intended not only for the saints in Ephesus, but sent around a circle of assemblies until it reached Laodicea. Paul, writing to the Colossians, said, "Read the epistle from Laodicea." Some think of this as a lost letter, but it is undoubtedly this letter to the Ephesians, and on account of its general character there are no personal salutations for individuals in the Ephesian church.

"Peace be to the brethren, and love with faith, from God the Father and the Lord Jesus Christ" —that peace which is the portion of all who have learned to commit everything to the care of our blessed Saviour. "Love," love for all saints, coupled with faith in the Lord Jesus Christ, the gift of God the Father in His blessed Son.

He closes with the characteristic Pauline salutation, "Grace be with all them that love our Lord Jesus Christ." And then he adds a very searching word at the very end, "in sincerity." The marginal translation is "in incorruptness." In other words, those who love our Lord Jesus Christ will manifest it by holy living. It is only thus we show in a practical way that we are one with Him in the heavenly places.